cook's library

Low Fat

cook's library

Low Fat

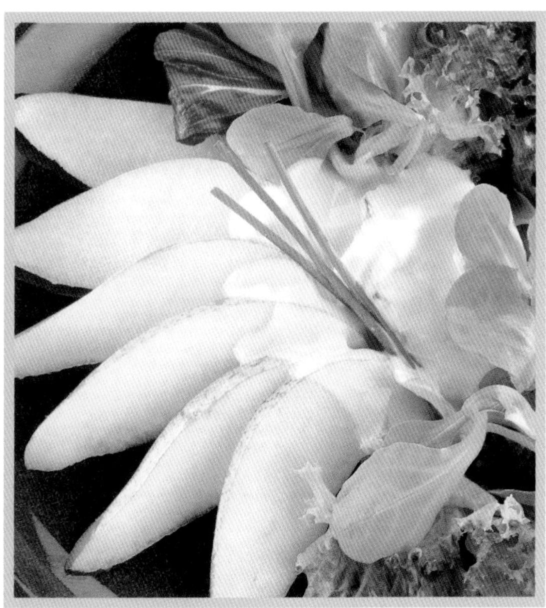

p

This is a Parragon Publishing Book
This edition published in 2004

Parragon Publishing
Queen Street House
4 Queen Street
Bath BA1 1HE, UK

Copyright © Parragon 2002

All rights reserved. No part of this publication may be reproduced, stored in a retrieval system, or transmitted, in any form or by any means, electronic, mechanical, photocopying, recordings, or otherwise, without the prior permission of the copyright holder.

ISBN: 0-75259-951-8

Printed in China

NOTE

Cup measurements in this book are for American cups. This book uses imperial and metric measurements. Follow the same units of measurement throughout; do not mix imperial and metric. All spoon measurements are level: teaspoons are assumed to be 5 ml, and tablespoons are assumed to be 15 ml. Unless otherwise stated, milk is assumed to be full fat, eggs and individual vegetables such as potatoes are medium, and pepper is freshly ground black pepper.

The times given for each recipe are an approximate guide only because the preparation times may differ according to the techniques used by different people and the cooking times may vary as a result of the type of oven used. The preparation times include chilling and marinating times, where appropriate.

Recipes using raw or very lightly cooked eggs should be avoided by infants, the elderly, pregnant women, convalescents, and anyone suffering from an illness.

Contents

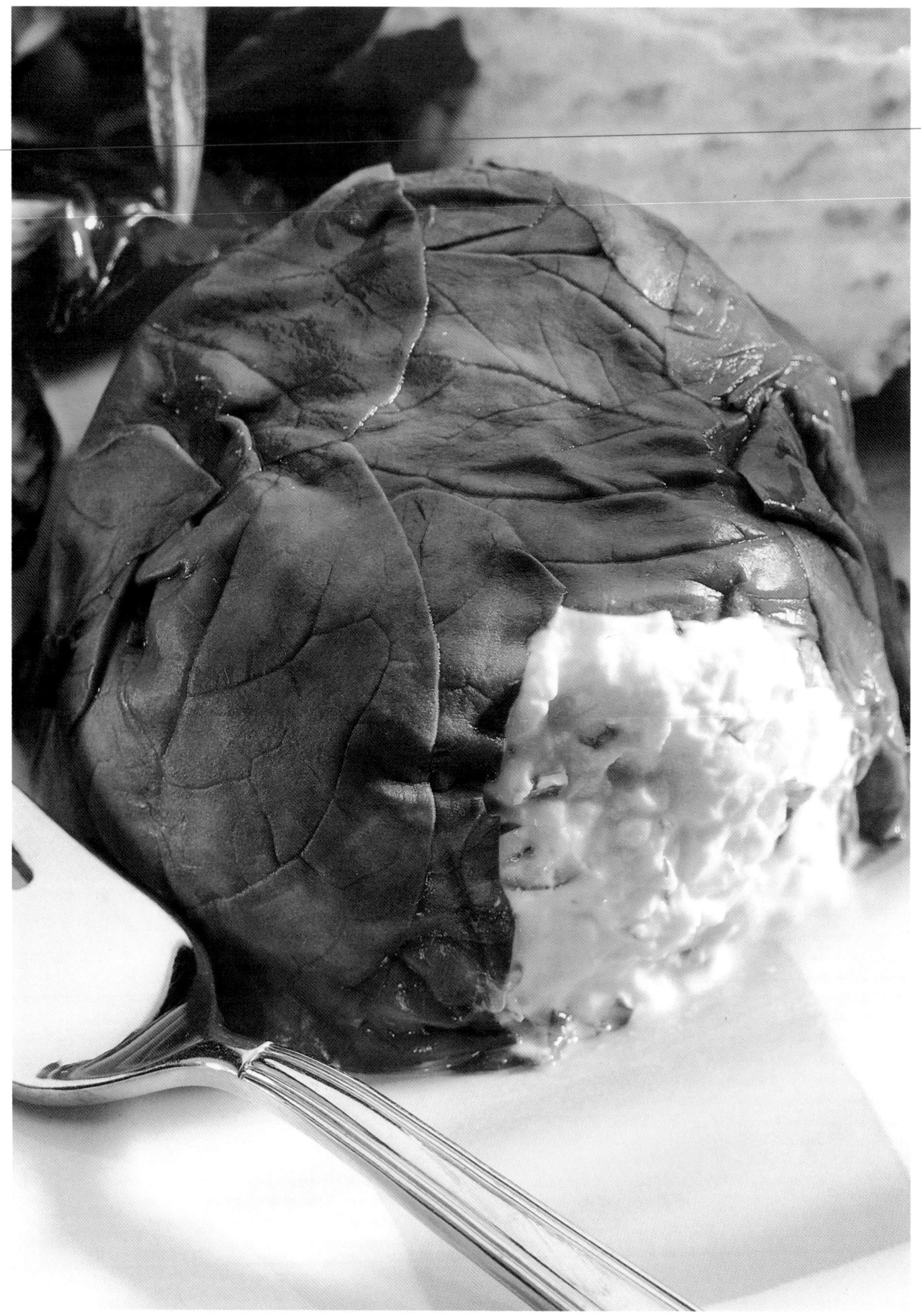

Introduction

Whether you follow a low-fat diet or simply want to introduce healthier eating habits to your lifestyle, this is the book for you. Although the majority of recipes are low in fat, some have been included because they are highly nutritious and add an important variety of ingredients.

Nutritionists agree that typical modern diets usually contain too much fat and that this can be detrimental to health. Yet, a moderate intake of fat is essential for good health. For example, the body requires fat-soluble vitamins. Fish oils are one of the richest sources of vitamins A and D, and vitamin E is found in vegetable oils. Fats are also a concentrated source of energy, providing over twice as much as carbohydrates or proteins. The aim should be to reduce fat in the diet, but not to cut it out altogether.

How much is too much?

The body's nutrient requirements, including the level of fat needed, vary with age, sex, general state of health, level of physical activity, and even genetic inheritance. However, the proportions in which the different nutrients are required are much the same from one person to another. The World Health Organization recommends that fats should not exceed 30 per cent of the daily intake of energy. (Energy is measured in calories, kilocalories or kilojoules.) It has conducted studies in countries with an exceptionally high rate of heart disease and the research has revealed that this almost invariably coincides with a high-fat diet, where fats comprise as much as 40 per cent of the body's daily energy intake.

If 2,000 calories a day is taken as the average, then, for good health, only 600 of them should be supplied by fats. One gram of pure fat yields nine calories, whereas one gram of pure carbohydrate or pure protein yields only one calorie. Simple arithmetic, therefore, indicates that the maximum daily intake of fats, based on a daily intake of 2,000 calories, should be 600 divided by nine, or 66.6 grams of fat.

Fats are broken down and digested in a different way from proteins and carbohydrate, and the human body is designed to store them for times of need. However, in the Western world, food is no longer scarce and we do not need to rely on stored fat to provide the energy for day-to-day life. If a lot of fat is stored, the body becomes overweight, even obese. Worse still, a mechanism that is not yet fully understood can suddenly trigger fat deposits in the arteries, resulting in their becoming narrower and eventually leading to heart disease.

Types of Fat

Anyone who is already overweight and is keen to return to a healthier size can reduce their fat intake to well below the 30 per cent maximum. However, it is probably better and the long-term effects will be more permanent if the overall intake of calories is reduced, but the proportions of nutrients remains within the normal range. Everyone, overweight or not, should observe the no more than 30 per cent rule to ensure long-term health and vitality.

Fats are made up of a combination of fatty acids and glycerol. Fatty acids consist of a chain of carbon atoms linked to hydrogen atoms. The way these are linked determines the type of fat—saturated or unsaturated. The type of fat you eat is just as important as the amount.

Saturated fats

Saturated fatty acids contain as many hydrogen atoms as possible—there are no empty links on the chain. They are mainly found in animal products, such as meat and dairy foods, although some vegetable oils, including palm and coconut oil, also contain them. Foods containing hydrogenated vegetable oils, such as some types of margarine, also contain saturated fats as a by-product of their processing. They are easy to recognize as they are usually solid at room temperature.

These are the fats that the body has difficulty processing and which it tends to store. They also increase cholesterol levels in the bloodstream, which may increase the risk of heart disease. It is, therefore, sensible to reduce the level of saturated fats in the diet. They should comprise no more than 30 per cent of the total fat intake or no more than nine per cent of the total energy intake.

Unsaturated fats

These fatty acids have spare links in the carbon chain and some hydrogen atoms are missing. There are two types: monounsaturated fats which have one pair of hydrogen atoms missing and polyunsaturated fats which have more than one pair missing. These fats are normally liquid or soft at room temperature. They are both thought to contribute to reducing the level of cholesterol in the bloodstream.

Monounsaturated fats are mainly of vegetable origin, but are also found in oily fish, such as mackerel. Other rich sources include olive oil, many kinds of nuts, and avocados. There are two types of polyunsaturated fats: omega 3 is found in oily fish and omega 6 in seeds and seed oils, such as sunflower.

Cholesterol

The word cholesterol is almost certain to be heard in the course of virtually any discussion about diet and health, yet its role in the human body is far from fully understood. Although increased levels of dietary and blood cholesterol have been linked with heart disease, this is not the full story.

Cholesterol is a sterol that is found in all animal fats and in some plants. It is also synthesized by the human liver from cholesterol-free substances, so it quite clearly serves some useful purpose. It seems to be important in the production of some of the body's natural steroids and a derivative is converted to vitamin D by the action of sunlight on the skin.

To complicate matters further, there are two types of proteins that carry cholesterol in the bloodstream: low-density and high-density lipoproteins. It seems that low-density lipoproteins promote atherosclerosis, the condition in which fats (lipids) are deposited on the inner walls of the arteries, narrowing them and constricting the flow of blood. This, in turn, increases the risk of heart attacks and heart disease. High-density lipoproteins, on the other hand, appear to retard atherosclerosis.

Research continues, but it is apparent that cholesterol is not always a villain. Its effects—good or bad—are controlled by other factors. It is probably more sensible, therefore, to think in terms of overall reduction of fat intake, especially saturated fats, than worry about the cholesterol content of individual foods.

Cooking Techniques

Frying

This is undoubtedly the technique that most dramatically raises the level of fats in the diet. You do not have to abandon chips or sausages completely, but it is sensible to make sure that they are only occasional treats rather than a staple diet. Fried-food fans might find it helpful to know that ingredients absorb much more fat when shallow-fried than they do during deep-frying, but even deep-frying should be used only occasionally. If you do enjoy a shallow-fried dish once in a while, invest in a good quality, heavy-based, non-slip skillet and you will require much less oil. Use a vegetable oil, high in polyunsaturates, for frying rather than a solid fat and measure the quantity you add to the pan. A spray oil is a useful way of controlling how much you use.

Try the Chinese cooking technique of stir-frying. The ingredients are cooked very rapidly over an extremely high heat, using a small amount of oil. Consequently, they absorb little fat and, as an additional advantage, largely retain their color, flavor, texture, and nutritional content.

Broiling

This is a good alternative to frying, resulting in foods with a similar crisp and golden coating, while remaining moist and tender inside. Ingredients with a delicate texture that can easily dry out, such as white fish or chicken breasts, will require brushing with oil, but more robust foods, such as red meat or oily fish, can usually be broiled without additional fat, providing the heat is not too fierce.

Consider marinating meat and fish in wine, soy sauce, cider, sherry, beer, and herbs or spices. Not only will the marinade tenderize meat and provide additional flavor, it can be brushed on during broiling, so that additional fat is not required. When broiling, always place the food on a rack, so that the fat drains away.

Poaching

This is an ideal technique for ingredients with a delicate texture or subtle flavor, such as chicken and fish, and is fat free. Poached food does not have to be bland and uninteresting. You can use all kinds of liquids, including bouillon, wine, and acidulated water, flavored with vegetables and herbs. The cooking liquid can be used as the basis for a sauce to provide additional flavor, as well as preserving any nutrients.

Steaming

A fat-free technique, steaming is becoming an increasingly popular way of cooking meat, fish, chicken, and vegetables. Ingredients retain their color, flavor, and texture, fewer nutrients leach out and it is a very economical method of cooking because steamers can be stacked on top of one another.

The addition of herbs and other flavorings to the cooking liquid, or the ingredients being steamed, also results in a wonderfully aromatic dish.

An additional advantage of steaming is that when meat is cooked, the fat melts and drips into the cooking liquid below. In this case, do not use the cooking liquid for making , bouillon, gravy, or sauces.

Braising and stewing

Slow-cooking techniques produce succulent dishes that are especially welcome during the winter. Trim all visible fat from the meat and always remove the skin from chicken. If red meat is to be browned first, consider dry-frying it in a heavy-based skillet or pan and drain off any fat before continuing with the recipe. Straining the cooking liquid, reducing it, and then skimming off the fat before serving is a classic way of preparing braised food and concentrates the flavor of the finished dish as well as reducing the fat content.

Roasting

Fat is an integral part of this cooking technique. Without it, meat or fish would dry out and become too brown. If you are planning a roast dish, stand meat on a rack over a tray or roasting pan so that the fat drains off. When making gravy, use bouillon or vegetable cooking water, rather than the meat juices.

Baking

Many baked dishes are virtually fat free. Foil- or baking paper-wrapped parcels of meat, fish, or vegetables are always delicious, since they help to retain any juices and nutrients. Add a little fruit juice, hard cider, wine, or sherry, rather than oil, butter, or margarine, for a moist texture and delicious flavor.

Basic Recipes

These recipes form the basis of several of the dishes contained throughout this book. Many of these basic recipes can be made in advance and stored in the refrigerator until required.

Fresh Chicken Bouillon

MAKES
7½ CUPS

2 lb 4 oz/1 kg chicken, skinned
2 celery stalks, chopped
1 onion, sliced
2 carrots, chopped
1 garlic clove
few fresh parsley sprigs
9 cups water
salt and pepper

1 Place all the ingredients in a large pan and bring to a boil.

2 Skim away any surface scum using a large, flat spoon. Reduce the heat to a gentle simmer, partially cover, and cook for 2 hours. Let cool.

3 Line a strainer with clean cheesecloth and place over a large pitcher or bowl. Pour the bouillon through the strainer. The cooked chicken can be used in another recipe. Discard the other solids. Cover the bouillon and chill.

4 Skim away any surface fat before using. Store in the refrigerator for up to 3 days, or freeze in small batches until required.

Fresh Vegetable Bouillon

MAKES
7½CUPS

1 large onion, sliced
1 large carrot, diced
1 celery stalk, chopped
2 garlic cloves
1 dried bay leaf
few fresh parsley sprigs
pinch of grated nutmeg
9 cups water
salt and pepper

1 Place all the ingredients in a large pan and bring to a boil.

2 Skim away any surface scum using a large, flat spoon. Reduce the heat to a gentle simmer, partially cover, and cook for 45 minutes. Let cool.

3 Line a strainer with clean cheesecloth and place over a large pitcher or bowl. Pour the bouillon through the strainer. Discard the solids.

4 Cover the bouillon and store in the refrigerator for up to 3 days, until required, or freeze in small batches.

Fresh Fish Bouillon

MAKES
7½ CUPS

2 lb 4 oz /1 kg white fish bones, heads and scraps
1 large onion, chopped
2 carrots, chopped
2 celery stalks, chopped
½ tsp black peppercorns
½ tsp grated lemon peel
few fresh parsley sprigs
9 cups water
salt and pepper

1 Rinse the fish trimmings in cold running water and place in a large pan with the other ingredients. Bring to a boil.

2 Skim away any surface scum using a large, flat spoon.

3 Reduce the heat to gentle simmer and cook, partially covered, for 30 minutes. Let cool.

4 Line a strainer with clean cheesecloth and place over a large pitcher or bowl. Pour the bouillon through the strainer. Discard the solids. Cover and store in the refrigerator for up to 3 days until required, or freeze in small batches.

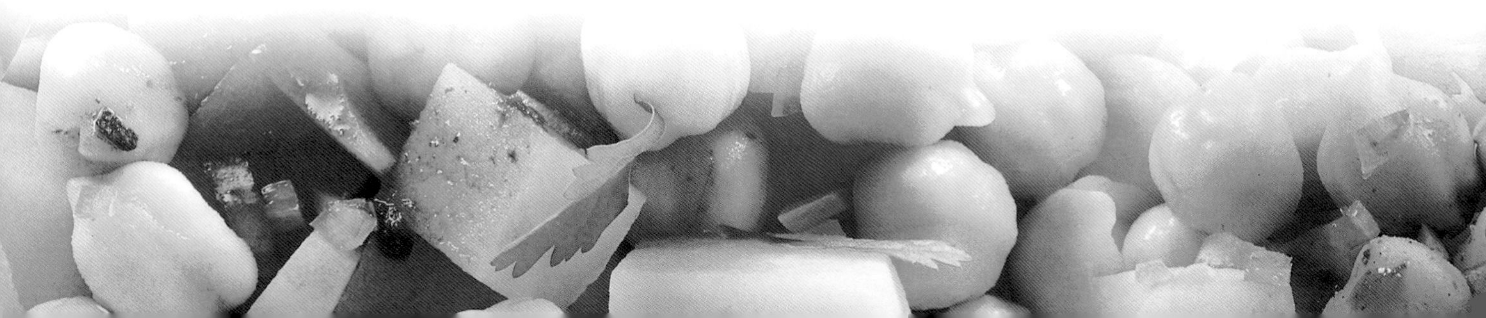

Fresh Beef Bouillon

MAKES
7½ CUPS

about 2 lb 4 oz/1 kg bones from a cooked joint or raw chopped beef
2 onions, studded with 6 whole cloves, or sliced, or chopped coarsely
2 carrots, sliced
1 leek, sliced
1–2 celery stalks, sliced
1 Fresh or Dry Bouquet Garni
10 cups water

1 Use chopped marrow bones with a few strips of shin of beef, if possible. Put in a roasting pan and cook in a preheated oven, 450°F/230°C, for 30–50 minutes, until browned.

2 Transfer to a large pan with the other ingredients. Bring to a boil and remove any scum from the surface with a large, flat spoon.

3 Cover and simmer gently for 3–4 hours. Strain the bouillon and let cool. Remove any fat from the surface and chill. If stored for more than 24 hours, the bouillon must be boiled every day, cooled quickly and chilled again.

4 The bouillon may be frozen for up to 2 months; place in a large plastic bag and seal, leaving at least 1-inch/2.5-cm of headspace to allow for expansion.

Chinese Bouillon

MAKES
10 CUPS

1 lb 10 oz /750 g chicken pieces, trimmed and chopped
1 lb 10 oz/750 g pork spare ribs
15 cups cold water
3–4 pieces of fresh gingerroot, chopped
3–4 scallions, each tied into a knot
3–4 tbsp Chinese rice wine or dry sherry

1 Place the chicken and pork in a large pan with the water. Add the ginger and scallions.

2 Bring to a boil, and skim away any surface scum using a large, flat spoon. Reduce the heat and simmer, uncovered, for at least 2–3 hours.

3 Strain the bouillon, discarding the chicken, pork, ginger, and scallions. Add the Chinese rice wine and return to a boil, then reduce the heat and simmer for 2–3 minutes. Let cool.

4 Refrigerate the bouillon when cool, it will keep for up to 4–5 days. Alternatively, it can be frozen in small batches and thawed as required.

Cornstarch Paste

Mix 1 part cornstarch with about 1.5 parts of cold water. Stir until smooth. The paste can be used to thicken sauces.

Fresh Bouquet Garni

1 fresh or dry bay leaf
few fresh parsley sprigs
few fresh thyme sprigs

Tie the herbs together with a length of string or cotton.

Dry Bouquet Garni

1 dry bay leaf
good pinch of dry mixed herbs or any one herb
good pinch of dry parsley
8–10 black peppercorns
2–4 cloves
1 garlic clove (optional)

Put all the ingredients in a small square of cheesecloth and secure with string or cotton, leaving a long tail so it can be tied to the handle of the pan for easy removal.

How to Use This Book

Each recipe contains a wealth of useful information, including a breakdown of nutritional quantities, preparation and cooking times, and level of difficulty. All of this information is explained in detail below.

A full-color photograph of the finished dish.

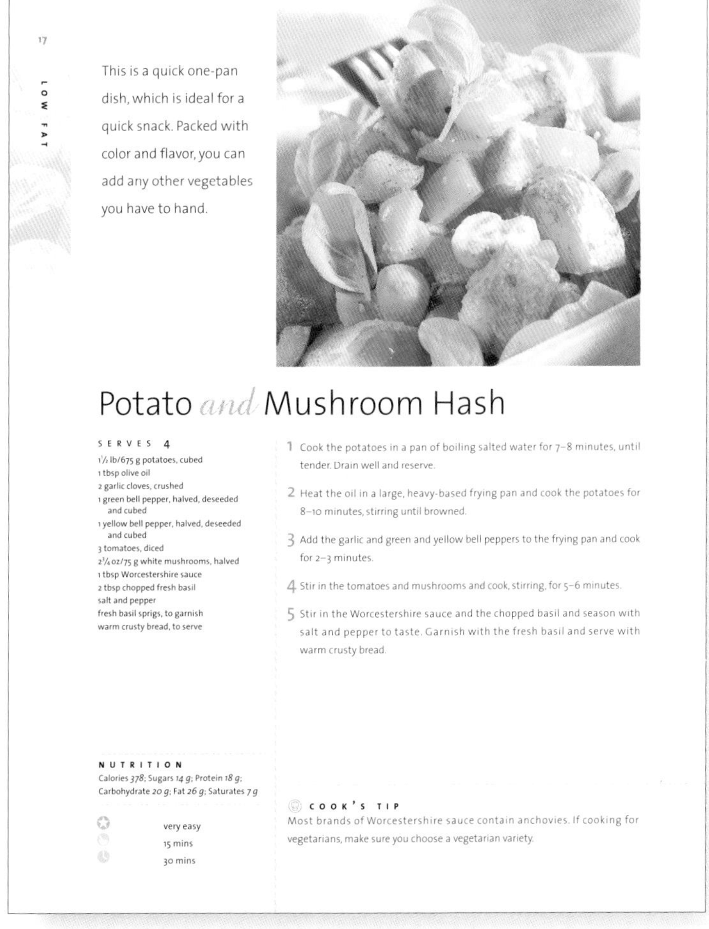

17

LOW FAT

This is a quick one-pan dish, which is ideal for a quick snack. Packed with color and flavor, you can add any other vegetables you have to hand.

Potato *and* Mushroom Hash

SERVES 4

1½ lb/675 g potatoes, cubed
1 tbsp olive oil
2 garlic cloves, crushed
1 green bell pepper, halved, deseeded and cubed
1 yellow bell pepper, halved, deseeded and cubed
3 tomatoes, diced
2¾ oz/75 g white mushrooms, halved
1 tbsp Worcestershire sauce
2 tbsp chopped fresh basil
salt and pepper
fresh basil sprigs, to garnish
warm crusty bread, to serve

1 Cook the potatoes in a pan of boiling salted water for 7–8 minutes, until tender. Drain well and reserve.

2 Heat the oil in a large, heavy-based frying pan and cook the potatoes for 8–10 minutes, stirring until browned.

3 Add the garlic and green and yellow bell peppers to the frying pan and cook for 2–3 minutes.

4 Stir in the tomatoes and mushrooms and cook, stirring, for 5–6 minutes.

5 Stir in the Worcestershire sauce and the chopped basil and season with salt and pepper to taste. Garnish with the fresh basil and serve with warm crusty bread.

NUTRITION

Calories 378; Sugars 14 g; Protein 18 g; Carbohydrate 20 g; Fat 26 g; Saturates 7 g

very easy
15 mins
30 mins

COOK'S TIP

Most brands of Worcestershire sauce contain anchovies. If cooking for vegetarians, make sure you choose a vegetarian variety.

The ingredients for each recipe are listed in the order that they are used.

The nutritional information provided for each recipe is per serving or per portion. Optional ingredients, variations or serving suggestions have not been included in the calculations.

The method is clearly explained with step-by-step instructions that are easy to follow.

Cook's tips provide useful information regarding ingredients or cooking techniques.

The number of stars represents the difficulty of each recipe, ranging from very easy (1 star) to challenging (4 stars).

This amount of time represents the preparation of ingredients, including cooling, chilling, and soaking times.

This represents the cooking time.

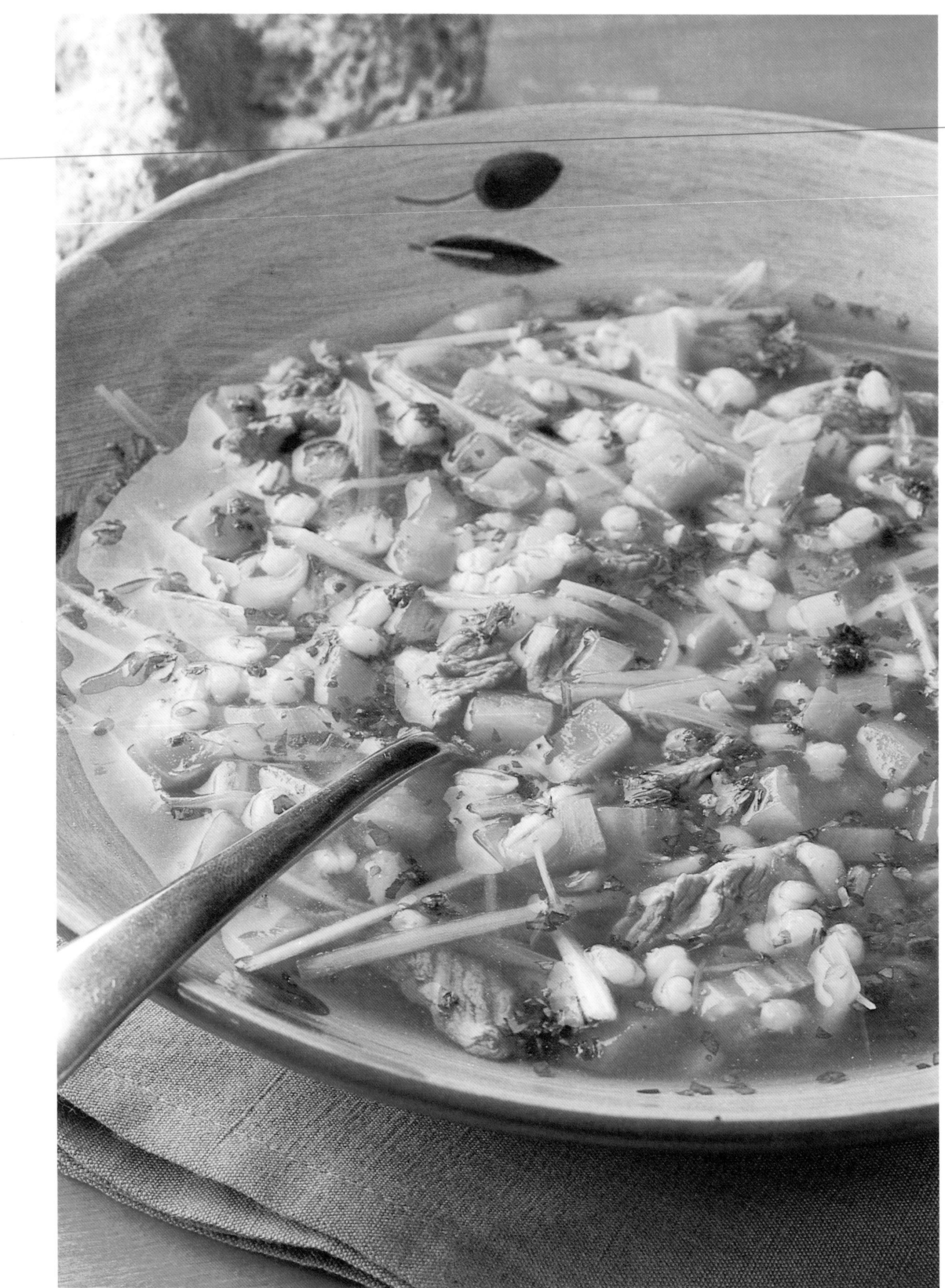

Soups

The traditional way to start a meal is with a soup, but they can also be a satisfying meal in themselves, depending on their ingredients, and if they are served with crusty bread. For best results use homemade bouillon, made from the liquor left after cooking vegetables and the juices from fish and meat. Ready-made bouillon in the form of bouillon cubes or granules tend to contain large amounts of salt and flavorings, which can overpower delicate flavors. Although making fresh bouillon takes a little longer, it is well worth it for the superior taste. It is a good idea to make a large batch and freeze the remainder, in smaller quantities, for later use. Potato can be added to thicken soups, rather than stirring in the traditional thickener of flour and water—or, worse, flour and fat.

This is a really hearty soup, filled with color, flavor, and goodness, which may be adapted to any vegetables that you have at hand.

Mixed Bean Soup

SERVES 4

1 tbsp vegetable oil
1 red onion, halved and sliced
3½ oz/100 g potato, diced
1 carrot, diced
1 leek, sliced
1 fresh green chile, sliced
3 garlic cloves, crushed
1 tsp ground coriander
1 tsp chili powder
4 cups Fresh Vegetable Bouillon (see page 14)
1 lb/450 g mixed canned beans, such as red kidney, borlotti, or small cannellini, drained and rinsed
salt and pepper
2 tbsp chopped fresh cilantro, to garnish

1 Heat the oil in a large pan and add the onion, potato, carrot, and leek. Cook, stirring occasionally, for 2 minutes, until the vegetables have slightly softened.

2 Add the chile and garlic and cook for another minute.

3 Stir in the ground coriander, chili powder, and the vegetable bouillon.

4 Bring the soup to a boil, reduce the heat, and cook for 20 minutes, or until the vegetables are tender.

5 Stir in the beans, season with salt and pepper to taste, and cook, stirring occasionally, for another 10 minutes.

6 Ladle the soup into bowls, garnish with chopped cilantro, and serve.

NUTRITION
Calories *190*; Sugars *9 g*; Protein *10g*; Carbohydrate *20 g*; Fat *4 g*; Saturates *0.5 g*

very easy
5 mins
45 mins

COOK'S TIP

Serve this soup with slices of warm corn bread or a cheese loaf.

This soup has a real Mediterranean flavor, using sweet red bell peppers, tomato, chile, and basil. It is great served with a warm olive bread.

Red Bell Pepper Soup

SERVES 4

8 oz/225 g red bell peppers, halved, seeded and sliced
1 onion, sliced
2 garlic cloves, crushed
1 fresh green chile, chopped
1¼ cups crushed tomatoes
2½ cups Fresh Vegetable Bouillon (see page 14)
2 tbsp chopped fresh basil
fresh basil sprigs, to garnish

1 Put the red bell peppers in a large pan with the onion, garlic, and chile. Add the crushed tomatoes and vegetable bouillon and bring to a boil over a medium heat, stirring constantly.

2 Reduce the heat and simmer for 20 minutes, or until the bell peppers have softened. Drain, reserving the liquid and vegetables separately.

3 Purée the vegetables by pressing through a strainer with the back of a spoon. Alternatively, process in a food processor to a smooth purée.

4 Return the vegetable purée to a clean pan and add the reserved cooking liquid. Add the basil and heat through until hot. Garnish the soup with fresh basil sprigs and serve.

NUTRITION

Calories *55*; Sugars *10 g*; Protein *2 g*; Carbohydrate *11 g*; Fat *0.5 g*; Saturates *0.1 g*

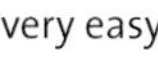

very easy
5 mins
25 mins

COOK'S TIP

This soup is also delicious served cold with ⅔ cup plain yogurt swirled into it.

Serve this soup over ice as a refreshing starter on a warm summer's day. It has the fresh tang of yogurt and a dash of spice from the Tabasco sauce.

Chilled Shrimp *and* Cucumber Soup

SERVES 4

- 1 cucumber, peeled and diced
- 1⅔ cups Fresh Fish Bouillon (see page 14), chilled
- ⅔ cup tomato juice
- ⅔ cup low-fat plain yogurt
- ⅔ cup low-fat fromage frais, or double the quantity of plain yogurt
- 4½ oz/125 g peeled, cooked shrimp, thawed if frozen, chopped roughly
- few drops of Tabasco sauce
- 1 tbsp chopped fresh mint
- salt and white pepper
- ice cubes, to serve

to garnish

- fresh mint sprigs
- cucumber slices
- whole, peeled shrimp

1 Place the cucumber in a blender or food processor and blend for a few seconds until smooth. (Alternatively, chop the cucumber finely and push through a strainer.)

2 Transfer the cucumber to a bowl. Stir in the bouillon, tomato juice, yogurt, fromage frais, if using, and shrimp, and mix well. Add the Tabasco sauce and season with salt and pepper to taste.

3 Stir in the chopped mint, cover and chill for at least 2 hours.

4 Ladle the soup into glass bowls and add a few ice cubes. Serve garnished with sprigs of fresh mint, cucumber slices and whole shrimp.

NUTRITION

Calories *83*; Sugars *7 g*; Protein *12 g*; Carbohydrate *7 g*; Fat *1 g*; Saturates *0.3 g*

easy

2 hrs 15 mins

0 mins

COOK'S TIP

Instead of shrimp, add white crab meat or cooked ground chicken. For a vegetarian version, omit the shrimp, add an extra 4½ oz/125 g cucumber, finely diced, and use Fresh Vegetable Bouillon (see page 14).

Although this chilled soup is not an authentic Indian dish, it is wonderful served as a "cooler" between hot, spicy courses.

Cucumber *and* Tomato Soup

SERVES 4

4 tomatoes, peeled and seeded
4-inch/10-cm piece of cucumber, peeled, seeded, and chopped
2 scallions, green parts only, chopped
3 lb 5 oz/1.5 kg watermelon, peeled and seeded
1 tbsp chopped fresh mint
salt and pepper
fresh mint sprigs, to garnish

1 Using a sharp knife, cut 1 tomato into ½-inch/1-cm dice.

2 Put the remaining 3 tomatoes into a blender or food processor and, with the motor running, add the cucumber, scallions, and watermelon. Process until smooth.

3 If not using a food processor, push the deseeded watermelon through a strainer. Stir the diced tomato and mint into the melon purée. Season with salt and pepper to taste. Finely chop the cucumber, scallions and the remaining 3 tomatoes and add to the melon.

4 Cover and chill the cucumber and tomato soup overnight in the refrigerator. Check the seasoning and transfer to a serving bowl. Garnish with fresh mint sprigs to serve.

NUTRITION

Calories *73*; Sugars *16 g*; Protein *2 g*; Carbohydrate *16 g*; Fat *1 g*; Saturates *0.2 g*

 easy

2 hrs

0 mins

COOK'S TIP

Although this soup does improve if chilled overnight, it is also delicious as a quick appetizer if whipped up just before a meal, and served immediately.

This tasty red lentil soup, flavored with chopped cilantro, can be easily made in the microwave. The yogurt adds a light piquancy to the soup.

Red Lentil Soup *with* Yogurt

SERVES 4

2 tbsp butter
1 onion, chopped finely
1 celery stalk, chopped finely
1 large carrot, grated
1 bay leaf
1 cup red lentils
5 cups hot Fresh Vegetable or Chicken Bouillon (see page 14)
2 tbsp chopped cilantro
4 tbsp low-fat plain yogurt
salt and pepper
fresh cilantro sprigs, to garnish

1 Place the butter, onion, and celery in a large bowl. Cover and cook in a microwave on High power for 3 minutes.

2 Add the carrot, bay leaf, and lentils. Pour in the bouillon. Cover and cook on High power for 15 minutes, stirring halfway through.

3 Remove the bowl from the microwave oven, cover, and stand for 5 minutes.

4 Remove and discard the bay leaf, then process, in batches, in a food processor, until smooth. Alternatively, press the soup through a strainer.

5 Pour the soup into a clean bowl. Season with salt and pepper to taste, and stir in the cilantro. Cover and cook on High power for 4–5 minutes, until the soup is piping hot.

6 Serve in warm soup bowls. Place 1 tablespoon of the yogurt on top of each serving and garnish with cilantro sprigs.

NUTRITION

Calories *280*; Sugars *6 g*; Protein *17 g*; Carbohydrate *40 g*; Fat *7 g*; Saturates *4 g*

easy

5 mins
30 mins

COOK'S TIP

For an extra creamy soup, try adding low-fat crème fraîche or sour cream instead of the yogurt.

This simple recipe uses the sweet potato with its distinctive flavor and color, combined with a hint of orange and cilantro.

Sweet Potato *and* Onion Soup

1 Heat the vegetable oil in a large pan and add the sweet potatoes, carrot, onions, and garlic. Sauté the vegetables over low heat, stirring constantly for 5 minutes, until softened.

2 Pour in the vegetable bouillon and orange juice and bring to a boil.

3 Reduce the heat, cover, and simmer the vegetables for 20 minutes, or until the sweet potatoes and carrot are tender.

4 Transfer the mixture to a food processor or blender, in batches, and process for 1 minute, until puréed. Return the purée to the rinsed-out pan.

5 Stir in the yogurt and chopped cilantro and season with salt and pepper to taste .

6 Serve the soup in warm soup bowls and garnish with cilantro sprigs and orange peel.

SERVES 4

2 tbsp vegetable oil
2 lb/900 g sweet potatoes, diced
1 carrot, diced
2 onions, sliced
2 garlic cloves, crushed
2½ cups Fresh Vegetable Bouillon (see page 14)
1¼ cups unsweetened orange juice
1 cup low-fat plain yogurt
2 tbsp chopped fresh cilantro
salt and pepper

to garnish

fresh cilantro sprigs
orange peel

NUTRITION

Calories *320*; Sugars *26 g*; Protein *7 g*; Carbohydrate *62 g*; Fat *7 g*; Saturates *1 g*

COOK'S TIP

This soup can be chilled before serving, if preferred. If chilling, stir the yogurt into the dish just before serving. Serve in chilled bowls.

 very easy

 15 mins

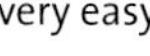 30 mins

Packed full of flavor, this delicious fish dish is really a meal in itself, but it is ideal accompanied by a crisp side salad.

Fish *and* Crab Chowder

SERVES 4

1 large onion, chopped finely
2 celery stalks, chopped finely
⅔ cup dry white wine
2½ cups Fresh Fish Bouillon (see page 14)
2½ cups skim milk
1 bay leaf
8 oz/225 g smoked cod fillet, skinned and cut into 1-inch/2.5-cm cubes
8 oz/225 g smoked haddock fillets, skinned and cut into 1-inch/2.5-cm cubes
12 oz/350 g canned crab meat, drained
8 oz/225 g green beans, sliced into 1-inch/2.5-cm pieces and blanched
1⅓ cups cooked brown rice
4 tsp cornstarch mixed with 4 tbsp water
salt and pepper
mixed salad greens, to serve

1 Place the onion, celery, and wine in a large, non-slip pan. Bring to a boil, cover, and cook over low heat for 5 minutes.

2 Uncover the pan and cook for a further 5 minutes, until almost all the liquid has evaporated.

3 Pour in the bouillon and milk and add the bay leaf. Reduce the heat, then stir in the cod and haddock. Simmer over low heat, uncovered, for 5 minutes.

4 Add the crab meat, beans, and cooked brown rice and simmer gently for 2–3 minutes, until just heated through. Remove the bay leaf with a draining spoon and discard.

5 Stir in the cornstarch mixture until the soup has thickened slightly. Season with salt and pepper to taste and ladle into warm soup bowls. Serve with mixed salad greens.

NUTRITION

Calories *440*; Sugars *10 g*; Protein *49 g*; Carbohydrate *43 g*; Fat *7 g*; Saturates *1 g*

easy

40 mins

30 mins

Carrot soup is very popular and here cumin, tomato, potato, and celery add both richness and depth.

Carrot *and* Cumin Soup

1 Melt the butter in a large pan. Add the onion and garlic and cook very gently until softened.

2 Add the carrots and cook gently for another 5 minutes, stirring frequently and taking care they do not brown.

3 Add the bouillon, cumin, celery, potato, tomato paste, lemon juice, and bay leaves and season with salt and pepper to taste, then bring to a boil. Reduce the heat, cover and simmer for about 30 minutes, until the vegetables are tender.

4 Remove and discard the bay leaves, cool the soup a little, and then press it through a strainer or process in a food processor or blender until smooth.

5 Pour the soup into a clean pan, add the milk, and bring to a boil over low heat. Taste and adjust the seasoning, if necessary.

6 Ladle into warm soup bowls, garnish with a small celery leaf and serve.

SERVES 4

3 tbsp butter or margarine
1 large onion, chopped
1–2 garlic cloves, crushed
12 oz/350 g carrots, sliced
3¾ cups Fresh Chicken or Vegetable Bouillon (see page 14)
¾ tsp ground cumin
2 celery stalks, thinly sliced
4 oz/115 g potato, diced
2 tsp tomato paste
2 tsp lemon juice
2 fresh or dried bay leaves
about 1¼ cups skim milk
salt and pepper
celery leaves, to garnish

NUTRITION

Calories *114*; Sugars *8 g*; Protein *3 g*; Fat *6 g*; Carbohydrate *12 g*; Saturates *4 g*

 moderate

15 mins

 45 mins

COOK'S TIP

This soup can be frozen for up to 3 months. Add the milk when reheating.

This nutritious soup uses split red lentils and carrots as its two main ingredients, and includes a selection of spices to give it a kick.

Spicy Dhal *and* Carrot Soup

SERVES 4

- 3/4 cup split red lentils, rinsed
- 5 cups Fresh Vegetable Bouillon (see page 14)
- 3 cups sliced carrots
- 2 onions, chopped
- 1 cup canned chopped tomatoes
- 2 garlic cloves, chopped
- 2 tbsp vegetable ghee or oil
- 1 tsp ground cumin
- 1 tsp ground coriander
- 1 fresh green chile, seeded and chopped, or 1 tsp minced chile
- 1/2 tsp ground turmeric
- 1 tbsp lemon juice
- salt
- 1 1/4 cups skim milk
- 2 tbsp chopped fresh cilantro
- plain yogurt, to serve

1 Place the lentils in a large pan with 2 1/2 cups of the bouillon, the carrots, onions, tomatoes, and garlic, then bring the mixture to a boil. Reduce the heat, cover, and simmer for 30 minutes, or until the vegetables and lentils are tender.

2 Meanwhile, heat the ghee or oil in a small pan. Add the ground cumin, ground coriander, chile, and turmeric and cook over low heat for 1 minute. Remove from the heat and stir in the lemon juice. Season with salt to taste.

3 Process the soup in batches in a blender or food processor. Return the soup to the pan, add the spice mixture and the remaining bouillon, and simmer over low heat for 10 minutes.

4 Add the milk, taste, and adjust the seasoning, if necessary. Stir in the chopped cilantro and reheat gently. Serve in warm soup bowls, garnished with a swirl of yogurt.

NUTRITION

Calories *173*; Sugars *11 g*; Protein *9 g*; Carbohydrate *24 g*; Fat *5 g*; Saturates *1 g*

 very easy

 15 mins

 45 mins

A slightly hot and spicy Indian flavor is given to this soup with the use of garam masala, chile, cumin, and cilantro.

Indian Potato *and* Pea Soup

1 Heat the vegetable oil in a large pan and add the potatoes, onion, and garlic. Sauté gently for about 5 minutes, stirring constantly.

2 Add the garam masala, ground coriander, and ground cumin, and cook for 1 minute, stirring all the time.

3 Stir in the vegetable bouillon and red chile and bring the mixture to a boil. Reduce the heat, cover and simmer for 20 minutes, until the potatoes begin to break down.

4 Add the peas and cook for another 5 minutes. Stir in the yogurt and season with salt and pepper to taste.

5 Pour into warm soup bowls. Garnish with the cilantro and serve hot with warm bread.

SERVES 4

2 tbsp vegetable oil
1¼ cups diced mealy potatoes
1 large onion, chopped
2 garlic cloves, crushed
1 tsp garam masala
1 tsp ground coriander
1 tsp ground cumin
3¾ cups Fresh Vegetable Bouillon (see page 14)
1 fresh red chile, chopped
¾ cup frozen peas
4 tbsp low-fat plain yogurt
salt and pepper
fresh cilantro, chopped, to garnish
warm bread, to serve

NUTRITION

Calories *153*; Sugars *8 g*; Protein *6 g*; Carbohydrate *18 g*; Fat *6 g*; Saturates *1 g*

very easy

15 mins

30 mins

COOK'S TIP

For slightly less heat, seed the chile before adding it to the soup. Always wash your hands after handling chiles because they contain volatile oils that can irritate the skin and make your eyes burn if you touch your face.

This comforting broth is perfect for a cold day and is just as delicious made with lean lamb or pork fillet.

Beef *and* Vegetable Soup

SERVES 4

2 oz /55 g pearl barley, soaked overnight
5 cups Fresh Beef Bouillon (see page 15)
1 tsp dried mixed herbs
8 oz/225 g lean rump or sirloin beef, trimmed and cut into strips
1 large carrot, diced
1 leek, shredded
1 onion, chopped
2 celery stalks, sliced
salt and pepper
2 tbsp chopped fresh parsley, to garnish
crusty bread, to serve

1 Place the pearl barley in a large pan. Pour the bouillon over and add the mixed herbs, then bring to a boil. Reduce the heat, cover and simmer gently over low heat for 10 minutes.

2 Skim away any scum that has risen to the top of the bouillon with a flat spoon.

3 Add the beef, carrot, leek, onion and celery to the pan. Bring back to a boil, cover and simmer for about 1 hour, or until the barley, meat and vegetables are just tender.

4 Skim away any remaining scum that has risen to the top of the soup with a flat spoon. Blot the surface with paper towels to remove any fat. Season with salt and pepper to taste.

5 Ladle the soup into warm soup bowls and sprinkle with parsley. Serve piping hot, accompanied with crusty bread.

NUTRITION

Calories *138*; Sugars *2 g*; Protein *13 g*; Carbohydrate *15 g*; Fat *3 g*; Saturates *1 g*

moderate
8 hrs 15 mins
1 hr 30 mins

COOK'S TIP

A vegetarian version can be made by omitting the beef and beef bouillon and using vegetable bouillon instead. Just before serving, stir in 6 oz/175 g fresh bean curd, drained and diced.

A traditional clear soup made from beef bones and lean ground beef. Thin strips of vegetables provide a colorful garnish.

Consommé

1 Put the bouillon and ground beef in a large pan. Leave for 1 hour. Add the tomatoes, carrots, onion, celery, turnip, if using, bouquet garni, 2 of the egg whites, the crushed shells of 2 of the eggs and season with plenty of salt and pepper. Bring to almost boiling point, whisking continuously with a flat whisk.

2 Cover and simmer for 1 hour, taking care not to allow the layer of froth on top of the soup to break.

3 Strain the soup through a jelly bag or scalded fine cloth, keeping the froth back until the last, then pour the ingredients through the cloth again into a clean pan. The resulting liquid should be clear.

4 If the soup is not quite clear, return it to the pan with another egg white and the crushed shells of 2 more eggs. Repeat the whisking process as before and then boil for 10 minutes; strain again.

5 Add the sherry, if using, to the soup and reheat gently. Place the garnish in the warm soup bowls and carefully pour in the soup. Serve with Melba toast.

SERVES 4

5 cups Fresh Beef Bouillon (see page 15)
8 oz/225 g ground extra lean beef
2 tomatoes, skinned, seeded, and chopped
2 large carrots, chopped
1 large onion, chopped
2 celery stalks, chopped
1 turnip, chopped (optional)
1 Fresh Bouquet Garni (see page 15)
2–3 egg whites
shells of 2–4 eggs, crushed
1–2 tbsp sherry (optional)
salt and pepper
Melba toast, to serve

to garnish

julienne strips of raw carrot, turnip, celery, or celery root or a one-egg omelette, cut into julienne strips

NUTRITION

Calories *109*; Sugars *6 g*; Protein *13 g*; Carbohydrate *7 g*; Fat *3 g*; Saturates *1 g*

 challenging

1 hr 30 mins

1 hr 15 mins

A mouth-watering, healthy, garlicky vegetable, bean and bacon soup. Serve it with granary or crusty whole-wheat bread.

Bacon, Bean, *and* Garlic Soup

SERVES 4

16–20 strips lean smoked back bacon
1 carrot, sliced thinly
1 celery stalk, sliced thinly
1 onion, chopped
1 tbsp oil
3 garlic cloves, sliced
3 cups hot Fresh Vegetable Bouillon (see page 14)
7 oz/200 g canned chopped tomatoes
1 tbsp chopped fresh thyme
14 oz /400 g canned cannellini beans, drained and rinsed
1 tbsp tomato purée
salt and pepper
grated colby cheese, to garnish

1 Chop 2 strips of the bacon and place in a bowl. Cook in a microwave on High power for 3–4 minutes, until the fat runs out and the bacon is well cooked. Stir the bacon halfway through cooking to separate the pieces. Transfer to a plate lined with paper towels and leave to cool. When cool, the bacon pieces should be crisp and dry.

2 Place the carrot, celery, onion, and oil in a large bowl. Cover and cook on High power for 4 minutes.

3 Chop the remaining bacon and add to the bowl with the garlic. Cover and cook on High power for 2 minutes.

4 Add the bouillon, chopped tomatoes, thyme, beans, and tomato purée. Cover and cook on High power for 8 minutes, stirring halfway through. Season with salt and pepper to taste. Ladle into warm soup bowls and sprinkle with the crisp bacon and grated cheese.

NUTRITION
Calories *261*; Sugars *5 g*; Protein *32 g*; Carbohydrate *25 g*; Fat *8 g*; Saturates *2 g*

easy
5 mins
20 mins

COOK'S TIP

For a more substantial soup add 2 oz/55 g small pasta shapes or short lengths of spaghetti with the bouillon and tomatoes. You will also need to add an extra ⅔ cup vegetable bouillon.

You can use either yellow or green split peas in this recipe, but both types must be well rinsed and soaked overnight before use.

Split Pea *and* Ham Soup

SERVES 4

1¼ cups dried yellow split peas, rinsed
7½ cups water
2 onions, chopped finely
1 small turnip,chopped finely
2 carrots, chopped finely
2–4 celery stalks, chopped finely
1 lean ham knuckle
1 Fresh Bouquet Garni (see page 15)
½ tsp dry thyme
½ tsp ground ginger
1 tbsp white wine vinegar
salt and pepper

1 Place the split peas in a bowl with half the water and let soak overnight.

2 Put the soaked peas and their liquor, the remaining water, the onions, turnip, carrots, and celery into a large pan, then add the ham knuckle, bouquet garni, dried thyme, and ginger and bring to a boil.

3 Remove any scum from the surface of the soup. Reduce the heat, cover and simmer gently for 2–2½ hours, until the peas are very tender.

4 Remove the ham knuckle and bouquet garni. Remove about 4½–6 oz/125–175 g meat from the knuckle and finely chop it.

5 Add the chopped ham and vinegar to the soup and season with salt and pepper to taste.

6 Bring back to a boil, then reduce the heat and simmer for 3–4 minutes before serving.

NUTRITION
Calories *323*; Sugars *9 g*; Protein *17 g*; Carbohydrate *45 g*; Fat *9 g*; Saturates *4 g*

 easy
 8 hrs 15 mins
2 hrs 45 mins

COOK'S TIP

If preferred, this soup can be strained or blended in a food processor or blender until smooth. You can vary the vegetables, depending on what is available. Leeks, celery root, or chopped tomatoes are particularly good.

This satisfying soup can be served as an entrée. You can add rice and bell peppers to make it even more hearty, as well as colorful.

Chicken *and* Leek Soup

SERVES 4

2 tbsp butter
12 oz/350 g skinless, boneless chicken, cut into 1-inch/2.5-cm pieces
12 oz/350 g leeks, cut into 1-inch/2.5-cm pieces
5 cups Fresh Chicken Bouillon (see page 14)
1 Dry Bouquet Garni (see page 15)
8 pitted prunes, halved
salt and white pepper

1 Melt the butter in a large pan, add the chicken and leeks, and cook for 8 minutes, stirring occasionally.

2 Add the chicken bouillon and bouquet garni to the mixture in the pan, and season with salt and pepper to taste.

3 Bring the soup to a boil, then reduce the heat and simmer over gentle heat for 45 minutes.

4 Add the pitted prunes and simmer for 20 minutes. Remove the bouquet garni sachet and discard. Pour the soup into warm soup bowls and serve.

NUTRITION
Calories *183*; Sugars *4 g*; Protein *21 g*; Carbohydrate *4 g*; Fat *9 g*; Saturates *5 g*

 very easy
 5 mins
 1 hr 15 mins

COOK'S TIP

Instead of the Dry Bouquet Garni, you can use a bunch of fresh, mixed herbs, tied together with string. Choose fresh herbs such as parsley, thyme, and rosemary.

This fragrant, Thai-style soup combines citrus flavors with coconut, and a hint of piquancy from the fresh chiles.

Chicken *and* Coconut Soup

1 Place the coconut in a heatproof bowl and pour the boiling water over.

2 Place a fine strainer over another bowl and pour in the coconut water. Work the coconut through the strainer with a back of a spoon.

3 Add the coconut water, chicken bouillon, scallions, and lemongrass to a large pan.

4 Add the lime peel, juice, gingerroot, soy sauce, and ground coriander to the pan.

5 Heat the bouillon to just below boiling point. Add the chicken and cilantro to the pan, then bring to a boil. Reduce the heat and simmer for 10 minutes.

6 Discard the lemongrass, lime peel, and chiles. Pour the blended cornstarch mixture into the saucepan and stir until slightly thickened. Season with salt and pepper to taste, then garnish with the chopped red chile.

SERVES 4

$1^3/_4$ cups unsweetened desiccated coconut
2 cups boiling water
2 cups Fresh Chicken Bouillon (see page 14)
4 scallions, thinly sliced
2 lemongrass stalks , outer leaves removed
sliced peel and juice of 1 lime
1 tsp fresh grated gingerroot
1 tbsp light soy sauce
2 tsp ground coriander
2 large fresh red chiles, bruised
12 oz/350 g cooked, skinless, boneless chicken breast, cut into thin strips
1 tbsp chopped fresh cilantro
1 tbsp cornstarch mixed with 2 tbsp cold water
salt and white pepper
chopped fresh red chile, to garnish

NUTRITION

Calories *345*; Sugars *2 g*; Protein *28 g*; Carbohydrate *5 g*; Fat *24 g*; Saturates *18 g*

 easy

15 mins

15 mins

Juicy chunks of fish and sumptuous shellfish are cooked in a flavorsome bouillon. Serve with toasted bread rubbed with garlic.

Mediterranean Fish Soup

SERVES 4

1 tbsp olive oil
1 large onion, chopped
2 garlic cloves, chopped finely
1¾ cups Fresh Fish Bouillon (see page 14)
⅔ cup dry white wine
1 bay leaf
1 sprig each of fresh thyme, rosemary, and oregano
1 lb/450 g firm white fish fillets, such as cod, monkfish, or halibut, skinned, and cut into 1-inch/2.5-cm cubes
1 lb/450 g fresh mussels, prepared
14 oz /400 g canned chopped tomatoes
8 oz/225 g peeled, cooked shrimp, thawed if frozen
salt and pepper
fresh thyme sprigs, to garnish

to serve
lemon wedges
4 slices toasted French stick, rubbed with a cut garlic clove

1 Heat the olive oil in a large pan and gently cook the onion and garlic for 2–3 minutes, until just softened.

2 Pour in the bouillon and wine and bring to a boil.

3 Tie the bay leaf and herbs together with clean string and add to the pan with the fish and mussels. Stir well, cover and simmer for 5 minutes.

4 Stir in the tomatoes and shrimp and continue to cook for another 3–4 minutes, until piping hot and the fish is cooked through.

5 Discard the herbs and any mussels that have not opened. Season with salt and pepper to taste, then ladle into warm soup bowls.

6 Garnish with fresh thyme sprigs and serve with lemon wedges and toasted bread.

NUTRITION
Calories *316*; Sugars *4 g*; Protein *53 g*; Carbohydrate *5 g*; Fat *7 g*; Saturates *1 g*

 moderate
30 mins
15 mins

Thai red curry paste is quite fiery, but adds a superb flavor to this soup. It is available in jars or packets from most super stores.

Coconut *and* Crab Soup

SERVES 4

1 tbsp peanut oil
2 tbsp Thai red curry paste
1 red bell pepper, halved, seeded, and sliced
$2\frac{1}{2}$ cups coconut milk
$2\frac{1}{2}$ cups Fresh Fish Bouillon (see page 14)
2 tbsp Thai fish sauce
8 oz/225 g canned or fresh white crab meat
8 oz/225 g fresh or frozen crab claws
2 tbsp chopped fresh cilantro
3 scallions, sliced

1 Heat the oil in a preheated wok or large, heavy-based pan, swirling it around to coat. Add the red curry paste and red bell pepper and cook over medium heat for 1 minute.

2 Add the coconut milk, bouillon, and fish sauce and bring to a boil.

3 Add the crab meat, crab claws, cilantro, and scallions.

4 Stir the mixture well and heat thoroughly for 2–3 minutes, or until all the ingredients are warmed through.

5 Transfer to warm soup bowls and serve hot.

NUTRITION
Calories *122*; Sugars *9 g*; Protein *11 g*; Carbohydrate 11 *g*; Fat *4 g*; Saturates *1 g*

 moderate
15 mins
 20 mins

COOK'S TIP

Clean the wok by washing it with water, using a mild detergent, if necessary, and a soft cloth or brush. Dry thoroughly, then wipe the surface with oil to protect it.

This traditional Scottish soup is thickened with a purée of rice and crabmeat cooked in milk. Add sour cream, if liked, at the end of cooking.

Partan Bree

SERVES 4

1 medium-sized boiled crab
1/2 cup long-grain rice
2 1/2 cups skimmed milk
2 1/2 cups Fresh Fish Bouillon (see page 14)
1 tbsp anchovy paste
2 tsp lime or lemon juice
1 tbsp chopped fresh parsley or 1 tsp chopped fresh thyme
3–4 tbsp sour cream (optional)
salt and pepper
snipped fresh chives, to garnish

1 Remove and reserve all the brown and white meat from the crab, then crack the claws and remove and chop the meat; reserve the claw meat.

2 Put the rice and milk into a saucepan and bring slowly to a boil. Reduce the heat, cover and simmer gently for about 20 minutes.

3 Add the reserved white and brown crabmeat, except the claw meat, and season with salt and pepper to taste, then simmer for another 5 minutes.

4 Let cool a little, then press through a strainer, or blend in a food processor or blender until smooth.

5 Pour the soup into a clean pan and add the bouillon and the reserved claw meat. Bring slowly to a boil, then add the anchovy paste and lime juice, and adjust the seasoning. Simmer for another 2–3 minutes.

6 Stir in the fresh parsley and then swirl sour cream, if using, on top of each serving. Garnish with fresh chives.

NUTRITION
Calories *112*; Sugars *5 g*; Protein *7 g*; Carbohydrate *18 g*; Fat *2 g*; Saturates *0.3 g*

easy
30 mins
35 mins

COOK'S TIP

If you are unable to buy a whole fresh crab, use about 6 oz/175 g frozen crabmeat and thaw thoroughly before use; or use 6 oz/175 g canned crabmeat and drain thoroughly.

Smoked haddock gives this soup a wonderfully rich flavor, while the mashed potatoes and yogurt thicken and enrich the bouillon.

Smoked Haddock Soup

1 Put the fish, onion, garlic, and water into a pan, then bring to a boil. Reduce the heat, cover, and simmer over low heat for 15–20 minutes.

2 Remove the fish from the pan. Strip off the skin and remove any bones, and reserve both. Flake the flesh finely with a fork.

3 Return the skin and bones to the cooking liquid and simmer for 10 minutes. Strain, discarding the skin and bones. Pour the cooking liquor into a clean pan.

4 Add the milk and flaked fish and season with salt and pepper to taste . Bring to a boil, then reduce the heat and simmer for about 3 minutes.

5 Gradually whisk in sufficient mashed potato to give a fairly thick soup, then stir in the butter, and add the lemon juice to taste.

6 Add the yogurt and 3 tablespoons of the chopped parsley. Reheat gently and adjust the seasoning, if necessary. Sprinkle with the remaining parsley and serve the soup immediately.

SERVES 4

8 oz/225 g smoked haddock fillet
1 onion, chopped finely
1 garlic clove, crushed
2½ cups water
2½ cups skim milk
2⅔–4 cups hot mashed potatoes
2 tbsp butter
about 1 tbsp lemon juice
6 tbsp low-fat plain yogurt
4 tbsp chopped fresh parsley
salt and pepper

NUTRITION

Calories *169*; Sugars *8 g*; Protein *16 g*; Carbohydrate *16 g*; Fat *5 g*; Saturates *3 g*

easy

25 mins

40 mins

Appetizers *and* Snacks

If you prefer not to start your meal with soup, then this chapter contains a range of appetizers to whet the appetite. There are low-fat appetizers from around the world, such as Thai Potato Cakes with chile and soy dipping sauce, or Sweet and Sour Drumsticks, which are grilled to give them a glossy glaze and are very low in fat. There are also attractive appetizers to impress your guests at a dinner party, for example, Turkey and Vegetable Loaf, and Spinach Cheese Molds. There is also a selection of pâtés, including Parsley, Chicken, and Ham and Smoked Fish and Potato, as well as snacks, including Spicy Garbanzos.

This is a quick one-pan dish, which is ideal for a quick snack. Packed with color and flavor, you can add any other vegetables you have at hand.

Potato *and* Mushroom Hash

SERVES 4

1 lb 8 oz/675 g potatoes, cubed
1 tbsp olive oil
2 garlic cloves, crushed
1 green bell pepper, halved, seeded, and cubed
1 yellow bell pepper, halved, seeded, and cubed
3 tomatoes, diced
1 cup halved white mushrooms
1 tbsp Worcestershire sauce
2 tbsp chopped fresh basil
salt and pepper
fresh basil sprigs, to garnish
warm crusty bread, to serve

1 Cook the potatoes in a pan of boiling salted water for 7–8 minutes, until tender. Drain well and reserve.

2 Heat the oil in a large skillet and cook the potatoes for 8–10 minutes, stirring until browned.

3 Add the garlic, and green and yellow bell peppers to the skillet and cook for 2–3 minutes.

4 Stir in the tomatoes and mushrooms and cook, stirring, for 5–6 minutes.

5 Stir in the Worcestershire sauce and the chopped basil and season with salt and pepper to taste. Garnish with the fresh basil and serve with warm crusty bread.

NUTRITION

Calories *378*; Sugars *14 g*; Protein *18 g*; Carbohydrate *20 g*; Fat *26 g*; Saturates *7 g*

 very easy

 15 mins

 30 mins

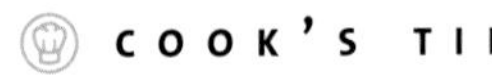

COOK'S TIP

Most brands of Worcestershire sauce contain anchovies. If cooking for vegetarians, make sure you choose a vegetarian variety.

This tasty dip is great for livening up simply cooked vegetables. Varying the vegetables according to the season adds interest to the dish.

Vegetables *with* Sesame Dip

1 Line the bottom of a steamer with baking parchment and arrange the broccoli, cauliflower, asparagus, and onion pieces on top.

2 Bring a large pan of water to a boil, and place the steamer on top. Sprinkle the vegetables with lime juice and steam for 10 minutes, or until they are just tender.

3 To make the dip, heat the oil in a small, non-slip pan, add the garlic, chili powder, and season with salt and pepper to taste, and cook gently for 2–3 minutes until the garlic is soft.

4 Remove the pan from the heat and stir in the sesame seed paste and yogurt. Return the pan to the heat and cook gently for 1–2 minutes without bringing to a boil. Stir in the chives.

5 Remove the vegetables from the steamer and place on a warm serving platter. Sprinkle them with the sesame seeds and garnish with chopped chives. Serve with the hot sesame seed dip.

SERVES 4

2½ cups small broccoli flowerets
2 cups small cauliflower flowerets
8 oz/225 g asparagus, sliced into 2-inch/5-cm lengths
2 small red onions, quartered
1 tbsp lime juice
2 tsp toasted sesame seeds
1 tbsp chopped fresh chives, to garnish

sesame seed dip

1 tsp sunflower oil
2 garlic cloves, crushed
½–1 tsp chili powder
2 tsp sesame seed paste (tahini)
⅔ cup low-fat plain yogurt
2 tbsp chopped fresh chives
salt and pepper

NUTRITION

Calories *126*; Sugars *7 g*; Protein *11 g*; Carbohydrate *8 g*; Fat *6 g*; Saturates *1 g*

easy

5 mins

20 mins

These flavor-packed little molds make a perfect appetizer or a tasty light lunch. Serve them with warm pitas.

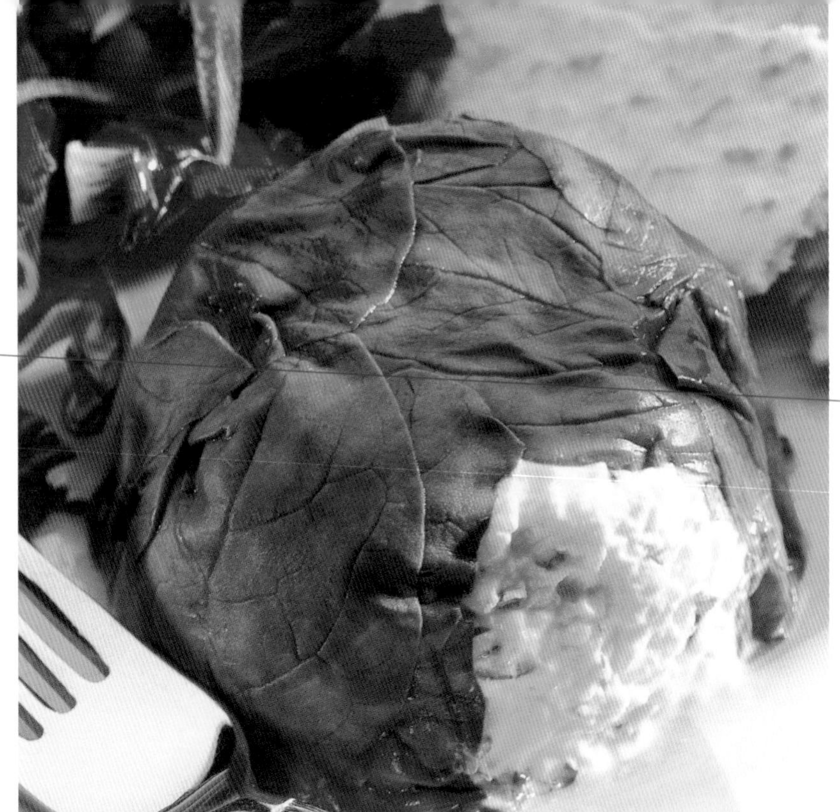

Spinach Cheese Molds

SERVES 4

3½ oz/100 g fresh spinach leaves, rinsed
10½ oz/300 g skim milk soft cheese
2 garlic cloves, crushed
fresh parsley, tarragon, and chive sprigs, chopped finely
salt and pepper

to serve
mixed salad greens and fresh herbs
warm pitas

1 Pack the spinach leaves into a pan while they are still wet, cover, and cook over a medium heat for about 3–4 minutes, until wilted—they will cook in the steam from the wet leaves (do not overcook). Drain well and pat dry with paper towels.

2 Line the bottom of 4 small heatproof bowls or individual ramekin dishes with baking parchment. Line the bowls or ramekins with the spinach leaves so that the leaves overhang the edges.

3 Place the cheese in a bowl and add the garlic and herbs. Mix together thoroughly and season with salt and pepper to taste.

4 Spoon the cheese and herb mixture into the bowls or ramekins and pull over the overlapping spinach to cover the cheese or lay extra leaves to cover the top. Place a waxed paper disc on top of each one and weigh them down with a 3½ oz/100 g weight. Cover with plastic wrap and refrigerate for 1 hour.

5 Remove the weights and peel off the waxed paper. Loosen the molds gently by running a small metal spatula around the edge of each mold and turn them out onto individual serving plates. Serve the molds immediately with a mixture of salad greens and fresh herbs, and warm pitas.

NUTRITION
Calories *119*; Sugars *2 g*; Protein *6 g*; Carbohydrate *2 g*; Fat *9 g*; Saturates *6 g*

 easy
1 hr 15 mins
5 mins

This pâté is easy to prepare and may be stored in the refrigerator for up to 2 days. Serve with small crispbread, Melba toast, or crudités.

Potato *and* Bean Pâté

1 Cook the potatoes in a pan of boiling water for 10 minutes, until tender. Drain well and mash.

2 Transfer the potato to a food processor or blender and add the beans, garlic, lime juice, and the cilantro.

3 Season with salt and pepper to taste and process for 1 minute to make a smooth purée. (Alternatively, mix the beans with the potato, garlic, lime juice, and cilantro and mash with a fork or a potato masher.)

4 Turn the pâté into a bowl and add the yogurt. Mix well.

5 Spoon the pâté into a serving dish and garnish with the cilantro sprigs. Serve at once or let chill.

SERVES 4

⅔ cup diced mealy potatoes
1½ cups mixed canned beans, such as borlotti beans, lima beans, and kidney beans, drained and rinsed
1 garlic clove, crushed
2 tsp lime juice
1 tbsp chopped fresh cilantro
2 tbsp low-fat plain yogurt
salt and pepper
fresh cilantro sprigs, to garnish

COOK'S TIP

To make Melba toast, toast bread lightly on both sides under a high broiler. Remove the crusts. Slide a sharp knife through the slice to split it horizontally. Cut into triangles and toast the untoasted side until the edges curl.

NUTRITION

Calories *84*; Sugars *3 g*; Protein *5.1 g*; Carbohydrate *15.7 g*; Fat *0.5 g*; Saturates *0.1 g*

easy

5 mins

10 mins

Although avocados do contain fat, it is unsaturated and if they are used in small quantities you can still enjoy their creamy texture.

Potato Skins *with* Guacamole

SERVES 4

4 large baking potatoes
2 tsp olive oil
coarse sea salt and pepper
chopped fresh chives, to garnish

guacamole dip

6 oz/175 g ripe avocado, skinned and pitted
1 tbsp lemon juice
2 ripe, firm tomatoes, chopped finely
1 tsp grated lemon peel
½ cup low-fat soft cheese with herbs and garlic
4 scallions, chopped finely
a few drops of Tabasco sauce
salt and pepper

1 Bake the potatoes in a preheated oven, 400°F/200°C, for 1¼ hours. Remove from the oven and let cool for 30 minutes. Reset the oven to 425°F/220°C.

2 Halve the potatoes lengthwise and scoop out 2 tablespoons of the flesh, then slice the potatoes in half again.

3 Place on a cookie sheet and brush the flesh side lightly with oil. Sprinkle with salt and pepper to taste. Bake for 25 minutes, until the potatoes are golden and crisp.

4 To make the guacamole dip, mash the avocado with the lemon juice. Add the remaining ingredients and mix.

5 Drain the potato skins on paper towels and transfer to a warm serving platter. Garnish with chives. Pile the avocado mixture into a serving bowl.

NUTRITION

Calories *399*; Sugars *4 g*; Protein *10 g*; Carbohydrate *59 g*; Fat *15 g*; Saturates *4 g*

easy

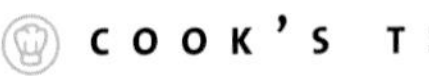
45 mins
1 hr 40 mins

COOK'S TIP

Mash the leftover potato flesh with low-fat plain yogurt and seasoning, and serve as an accompaniment.

A great texture and flavor are achieved by mixing white and granary flours with minced onion, grated cheese, and fresh herbs.

Cheese, Herb, *and* Onion Rolls

1 Strain the white flour with the salt, mustard, and pepper into a large bowl. Mix in the granary flour, herbs, scallions, and most of the cheese.

2 Blend the fresh yeast with the warm water or, if using dry yeast, dissolve the sugar in the water, sprinkle the yeast on top, and let stand in a warm place for about 10 minutes, until foamy. Add the yeast mixture to the dry ingredients and mix to form a firm dough, adding more flour, if necessary.

3 Knead until smooth and elastic. Cover with an oiled plastic bag and let rise in a warm place for 1 hour, or until doubled in size. Knock back and knead the dough until smooth. Divide into 10–12 pieces and shape into round or long rolls, coils, or knots.

4 Alternatively, make 1 large plaited loaf. Divide the dough into 3 even pieces and roll each into a long, thin sausage and join at one end. Beginning at the joined end, plait to the end and secure. Place on greased cookie sheets, cover with an oiled sheet of plastic wrap, and let rise until doubled in size. Remove the plastic wrap.

5 Sprinkle the rolls of loaf with the rest of the cheese. Bake in a preheated oven, 400°F/200°C for 15–20 minutes, for the rolls, or 30–40 minutes, for the loaf.

SERVES 4

1½ cups strong white flour
1½ tsp salt
1 tsp dried mustard powder
good pinch of pepper
1¾ cups Granary or malted wheat flour
2 tbsp chopped fresh mixed herbs
2 tbsp chopped finely scallions
1–1½ cups grated low-fat sharp colby cheese
15 g/½ oz fresh yeast; or 1½ tsp dry yeast plus 1 tsp caster sugar, or 1 package rapid-rise dry yeast plus 1 tbsp oil
1¼ cups warm water

NUTRITION

Calories *529*; Sugars *2 g*; Protein *24 g*; Carbohydrate *98 g*; Fat *7 g*; Saturates *4 g*

 moderate

 1 hr 30 mins

20–40 mins

These tea-time classics have been given a healthy twist by the use of low-fat soft cheese and reduced-fat colby cheese.

Cheese *and* Chive Biscuits

SERVES 4

generous 1½ cups self-rising flour
1 tsp powdered mustard
½ tsp cayenne pepper
½ tsp salt
½ cup low-fat soft cheese with added herbs
2 tbsp snipped fresh chives, plus extra to garnish
scant ½ cup skim milk, plus 2 tbsp for brushing
generous ½ cup grated reduced-fat sharp colby cheese
low-fat soft cheese, to serve

1 Strain the flour, mustard, cayenne pepper, and salt into a mixing bowl.

2 Add the soft cheese to the mixture and mix together until well incorporated. Stir in the snipped chives.

3 Make a well in the center of the ingredients and gradually pour in the milk, stirring, until the mixture forms a soft dough.

4 Turn the dough out onto a floured counter and knead lightly. Roll out until ¾-inch/2-cm thick, and use a 2-inch/5-cm plain dough cutter to stamp out as many circles as you can. Transfer the circles to a cookie sheet.

5 Reknead the dough trimmings together and roll out again. Stamp out more circles—you should be able to make 10 biscuits in total.

6 Brush the biscuits with the remaining milk and sprinkle with the grated cheese. Bake in a preheated oven, 400°F/200°C, for 15–20 minutes, until risen and golden.

7 Transfer to a wire rack to cool. Serve warm with low-fat soft cheese, garnished with chives.

NUTRITION

Calories *297*; Sugars *3 g*; Protein *13 g*; Carbohydrate *49 g*; Fat *7 g*; Saturates *4 g*

 easy

10 mins

20 mins

COOK'S TIP

For sweet biscuits, omit the mustard, cayenne pepper, chives, and grated cheese. Replace the flavored soft cheese with plain low-fat soft cheese. Add ½ cup currants and 2 tablespoons of superfine sugar in step 2.

You can use dried garbanzo beans, soaked overnight, for this popular Indian snack, but the canned variety is just as flavorsome.

Spicy Garbanzo Bean Snack

1 Place the potatoes in a pan, add enough water to cover, and bring to a boil. Reduce the heat, cover and simmer over a medium heat for 10 minutes, until cooked through. Test by inserting the tip of a knife into the potatoes—they should feel soft and tender. Drain and set aside.

2 Put the garbanzo beans into a bowl.

3 Combine the tamarind paste and water in a separate bowl. Add the chili powder, sugar, and 1 teaspoon salt and mix again. Pour the mixture over the garbanzo beans.

4 Add the onion and the potatoes to the garbanzo beans and stir to mix, taking care not to break up the potatoes. Season with pepper to taste .

5 Transfer to a serving bowl and garnish with tomatoes, if using, chiles and fresh cilantro leaves.

SERVES 4

2 potatoes, diced
14 oz/400 g canned garbanzo beans, drained and rinsed
2 tbsp tamarind paste
6 tbsp water
1 tsp chili powder
2 tsp sugar
1 onion, chopped finely
salt and pepper

to garnish

1 tomato, sliced (optional)
2 fresh green chiles, chopped
fresh cilantro leaves

COOK'S TIP

Garbanzo beans have a nutty flavor and slightly crunchy texture. Indian cooks also grind these to make a flour called gram or besan, which is used to make breads, thicken sauces, and to make batters for deep-fried dishes.

NUTRITION

Calories *190*; Sugars *4 g*; Protein *9 g*; Carbohydrate *34 g*; Fat *3 g*; Saturates *0.3 g*

easy

5 mins

15 mins

Spanish onions are ideal for this recipe, as they have a mild, sweet flavor that is not too overpowering.

Baked Stuffed Onions

SERVES 4

4 large Spanish onions
2 strips streaky bacon, diced
½ red bell pepper, seeded and diced
4½ oz/125 g ground lean beef
1 tbsp chopped mixed fresh herbs, such as parsley, thyme and rosemary or 1 tsp dry mixed herbs
½ cup fresh white breadcrumbs
1¼ cups Fresh Beef Bouillon (see page 15)
salt and pepper
long-grain rice, to serve
chopped fresh parsley, to garnish

gravy

2 tbsp butter
1¾ cups chopped finely white mushrooms
1¼ cups Fresh Beef Bouillon (see page 15)
2 tbsp cornstarch
2 tbsp water

NUTRITION

Calories *182*; Sugars *6 g*; Protein *10 g*; Carbohydrate *18 g*; Fat *9 g*; Saturates *5 g*

 moderate
15 mins
2 hrs 15 mins

1 Put the onions in a pan of lightly salted water. Bring to a boil, then reduce the heat and simmer for 15 minutes, until tender.

2 Remove the onions from the pan, drain and cool slightly, then hollow out the centers and finely chop.

3 Heat a skillet and cook the bacon until the fat runs out. Add the chopped onion and red bell pepper, and cook for 5–7 minutes, stirring frequently.

4 Add the beef to the skillet and cook, stirring, for 3 minutes, until browned. Remove from the heat and stir in the herbs, breadcrumbs, and season with salt and pepper to taste.

5 Grease an ovenproof dish and stand the whole onions in it. Pack the beef mixture into the centers and pour the bouillon around them.

6 Bake the stuffed onions in a preheated oven, 350°F/180°C, for 1–1½ hours, or until tender.

7 To make the gravy, heat the butter in a small pan and cook the mushrooms for 3–4 minutes. Strain the liquid from the onions and add to the pan with the bouillon, then cook for 2–3 minutes.

8 Mix the cornstarch with the water, then stir it into the gravy and heat, stirring, until thickened and smooth. Season with salt and pepper to taste. Serve the onions with the gravy and rice, garnished with fresh parsley.

This delicious smoked fish pâté is given a tart, fruity flavor by the gooseberries, which complement the fish perfectly.

Smoked Fish *and* Potato Pâté

1 Cook the potatoes in a pan of boiling water for 10 minutes, until tender, then drain well.

2 Place the cooked potatoes in a food processor or blender.

3 Add the smoked mackerel and process for 30 seconds, until fairly smooth. Alternatively, place the ingredients in a bowl and mash with a fork.

4 Add the cooked gooseberries, lemon juice, and crème fraîche to the fish and potato mixture. Blend for a further 10 seconds, or mash well.

5 Stir in the capers, gherkin, dill pickle, and fresh dill. Season with salt and pepper to taste.

6 Spoon the fish pâté into a serving dish, garnish with lemon wedges and serve with slices of warm crusty bread.

SERVES 4

1 lb 7 oz/650 g mealy potatoes, diced
10½ oz/300 g smoked mackerel, skinned and flaked
3 oz/85 g cooked gooseberries
2 tsp lemon juice
2 tbsp low-fat crème fraîche
1 tbsp capers, rinsed
1 gherkin, chopped
1 tbsp chopped dill pickle
1 tbsp chopped fresh dill
salt and pepper
lemon wedges, to garnish
warm crusty bread, to serve

NUTRITION

Calories *418*; Sugars *4 g*; Protein *18 g*; Carbohydrate *32 g*; Fat *25 g*; Saturates *6 g*

  easy

 20 mins

10 mins

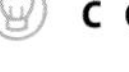 **COOK'S TIP**

Use stewed, canned, or bottled cooked gooseberries for convenience and to save time, or when fresh gooseberries are out of season.

These crab cakes are based on a traditional Thai recipe. They make a delicious snack when served with this sweet and sour cucumber sauce.

Thai Potato Crab Cakes

SERVES 4

1 lb/450 g mealy potatoes, diced
6 oz/175 g white crabmeat, drained if canned
4 scallions, chopped
1 tsp light soy sauce
½ tsp sesame oil
1 tsp chopped lemongrass
1 tsp lime juice
3 tbsp all-purpose flour
2 tbsp vegetable oil
salt and pepper

sauce

4 tbsp chopped finely cucumber
2 tbsp honey
1 tbsp garlic wine vinegar
½ tsp light soy sauce
1 fresh red chile, chopped

to garnish

1 fresh red chile, sliced
cucumber slices

1 Cook the potatoes in a pan of boiling water for 10 minutes, until cooked through. Drain well and mash.

2 Mix the crabmeat into the potato with the scallions, soy sauce, sesame oil, lemongrass, lime juice, and flour. Season with salt and pepper to taste.

3 Divide the crab and potato mixture into 8 equal portions and shape them into small rounds, using floured hands.

4 Heat the oil in a preheated wok or large, heavy-based skillet and cook the cakes, in batches of 4 at a time, for 5–7 minutes, turning once. Remove from the pan with a spatula. Drain on paper towels and keep warm.

5 Meanwhile, make the dipping sauce. In a small serving bowl, mix together the cucumber, honey, vinegar, soy sauce, and chile.

6 Garnish the cakes with the red chile and cucumber slices and serve with the dipping sauce.

NUTRITION

Calories *254*; Sugars *9 g*; Protein *12 g*; Carbohydrate *40 g*; Fat *6 g*; Saturates *1 g*

easy
15 mins
25 mins

COOK'S TIP

When using lemongrass, remove the tough outer leaves and the root and finely chop.

Broiled mixed sweet bell peppers are filled with tender tuna, corn, nutty brown and wild rice, and grated, reduced-fat cheese.

Rice *and* Tuna Bell Peppers

1 Place the wild rice and brown rice in separate pans, cover with boiling water, and bring back to a boil. Cook for about 40–50 minutes, or according to the package instructions. Strain the rice well.

2 Meanwhile, preheat the broiler to medium. Arrange the bell peppers on the broiler rack, cut side down. Cook for 5 minutes, turn over, and cook for another 4–5 minutes.

3 Combine the cooked rices in a large bowl and add the flaked tuna and drained corn. Gently fold in the grated cheese. Stir the basil leaves into the rice mixture and season with salt and pepper to taste.

4 Divide the tuna and rice mixture into 8 equal portions. Pile each portion into each cooked bell pepper half. Combine the bread crumbs and Parmesan cheese and sprinkle the mixture over each bell pepper.

5 Place the bell peppers under the broiler again for 4–5 minutes, until hot and golden brown.

6 Serve the bell peppers immediately, garnished with basil and accompanied with fresh, crisp salad greens.

SERVES 4

¼ cup wild rice
¼ cup brown rice
4 assorted bell peppers, halved and seeded
7 oz/200 g canned tuna in brine, drained and flaked
11½ oz/325 g canned corn kernels, drained
scant 1 cup grated reduced-fat sharp Colby cheese
1 bunch fresh basil leaves, shredded
2 tbsp dry white bread crumbs
1 tbsp freshly grated Parmesan cheese
salt and pepper
fresh basil leaves, to garnish
crisp salad greens, to serve

NUTRITION

Calories *332*; Sugars *13 g*; Protein *27 g*; Carbohydrate *42 g*; Fat *8 g*; Saturates *4 g*

 moderate

 10 mins

1 hr 5 mins

This impressive-looking turkey loaf is flavored with herbs and a layer of juicy tomatoes, then covered with ribbons of zucchini.

Turkey *and* Vegetable Loaf

SERVES 4

1 onion, chopped finely
1 garlic clove, crushed
2 lb/900 g lean ground turkey
1 tbsp chopped fresh parsley
1 tbsp chopped fresh chives
1 tbsp chopped fresh tarragon
1 egg white, beaten lightly
2 zucchini, 1 medium, 1 large
2 tomatoes, sliced thinly
salt and pepper
tomato and herb sauce, to serve

1 Preheat the oven to 375°F/190°C and line a non-stick loaf pan with baking parchment. Place the onion, garlic, and turkey in a bowl. Add the herbs,and season with salt and pepper to taste. Mix together with your hands, then add the egg white to bind.

2 Press half of the turkey mixture into the bottom of the pan. Thinly slice the medium zucchini and arrange with the tomatoes over the meat. Top with the rest of the turkey mixture and press down firmly.

3 Cover with a layer of kitchen foil and place in a roasting pan. Pour in enough boiling water to come half-way up the sides of the loaf pan. Bake in the oven for 1–1¼ hours, removing the foil for the last 20 minutes of cooking. Test the loaf is cooked by inserting a skewer into the center—the juices should run clear. The loaf will also shrink away from the sides of the pan.

4 Meanwhile, using a vegetable peeler or hand-held metal cheese slicer, cut the zucchini into thin slices. Bring a pan of water to a boil and blanch the zucchini ribbons for 1–2 minutes, until just tender. Drain and keep warm.

5 Remove the turkey loaf from the pan and transfer to a warm platter. Drape the zucchini ribbons over the turkey loaf and serve with a tomato and herb sauce.

NUTRITION
Calories *165*; Sugars *1 g*; Protein *36 g*; Carbohydrate *1 g*; Fat *2 g*; Saturates *0.5 g*

 easy
10 mins
1 hr 20 mins

This recipe is bound to be popular with children and is very easy to prepare for their supper.

Cranberry Turkey Burgers

1 Combine the turkey, onion, sage, bread crumbs, and cranberry sauce and season with salt and pepper to taste , then bind with egg white.

2 Press into 4 x 4-inch/10-cm rounds, about 3/4-inch/2-cm thick. Chill the burgers for 30 minutes.

3 Line a broiler rack with baking paper, making sure the ends are secured underneath the rack to ensure they don't catch fire. Place the burgers on top and brush lightly with oil. Put under a preheated moderate broiler and cook for 10 minutes. Turn the burgers over, brush again with oil, then cook for another 12–15 minutes, until cooked through.

4 Fill the burger rolls with lettuce, tomato, and a burger and top with cranberry sauce.

SERVES 4

12 oz/350 g ground lean turkey
1 onion, chopped finely
1 tbsp chopped fresh sage
6 tbsp dry white bread crumbs
4 tbsp cranberry sauce
1 egg white, beaten lightly
2 tsp sunflower oil
salt and pepper

to serve

4 toasted whole-wheat burger rolls
½ lettuce, shredded
4 tomatoes, sliced
4 tsp cranberry sauce

NUTRITION

Calories *209*; Sugars *15 g*; Protein *22 g*; Carbohydrate *21 g*; Fat *5 g*; Saturates *1 g*

 easy

45 mins

25 mins

COOK'S TIP

Look out for a variety of ready ground meats at your butchers or super store. If unavailable, you can grind your own by choosing lean cuts and processing them in a blender or food processor.

Pâté is easy to make at home, and this combination of lean chicken, ham, and herbs is especially straightforward.

Parsley, Chicken, *and* Ham Pâté

SERVES 4

8 oz/225 g skinless, boneless lean chicken, cooked and diced
3½ oz/100 g lean ham
small bunch of fresh parsley
1 tsp grated lime peel, plus extra to garnish
2 tbsp lime juice
1 garlic clove, peeled
½ cup low-fat cream cheese
salt and pepper

to serve
lime wedges
crispbread or Melba toast
mixed salad greens

1 Place the chicken and ham in a blender or food processor.

2 Add the parsley, lime peel and juice, and garlic and process until finely ground. (Alternatively, finely chop the chicken, ham, parsley, and garlic and place in a bowl. Gently stir in the lime peel and lime juice.)

3 Transfer the mixture to a bowl and stir in the cream cheese. Season with salt and pepper to taste, cover with plastic wrap, and chill in the refrigerator for about 30 minutes.

4 Spoon the pâté into individual serving dishes and garnish with extra grated lime peel. Serve the pâté with lime wedges, crispbread, and fresh salad greens.

NUTRITION

Calories *119*; Sugars *2 g*; Protein *20 g*; Carbohydrate *2 g*; Fat *3 g*; Saturates *1 g*

very easy

45 mins

0 mins

COOK'S TIP

This pâté can be made successfully with other kinds of ground, lean, cooked meat, such as turkey, beef, or pork. Alternatively, replace the meat with peeled shrimp and/or white crabmeat, or with canned tuna in brine, drained.

Chicken drumsticks are marinated to impart a tangy, sweet-and-sour flavor and a shiny glaze before being cooked on a barbecue grill.

Sweet *and* Sour Drumsticks

1 Skin the chicken drumsticks, if desired, and slash 2–3 times with a sharp knife. Put the chicken drumsticks into a nonmetallic shallow dish, arranging them in a single layer.

2 Combine the vinegar, tomato paste, soy sauce, honey, Worcestershire sauce, and garlic in a bowl. Season with cayenne pepper, and salt, and pepper to taste . Pour the mixture over the chicken, turning to coat. Cover and set aside in the refrigerator to marinate for 1 hour.

3 Cook the drumsticks on a hot barbecue grill or under a preheated broiler for about 20 minutes, brushing with the glaze several times during cooking, until the chicken is golden and the juices run clear when the thickest part is pierced with a skewer.

4 Transfer the drumsticks to a warm serving dish and serve immediately with crisp salad greens.

SERVES 4

8 chicken drumsticks
4 tbsp red wine vinegar
2 tbsp tomato paste
2 tbsp soy sauce
2 tbsp honey
1 tbsp Worcestershire sauce
1 garlic clove, crushed
pinch of cayenne pepper
salt and pepper
mixed salad greens, to serve

NUTRITION

Calories *171*; Sugars *9 g*; Protein *23 g*; Carbohydrate *10 g*; Fat *5 g*; Saturates *1 g*

very easy

1 hr 15 mins

20 mins

COOK'S TIP

For a tangy flavor, add the juice of 1 lime to the marinade. While the drumsticks are cooking, check regularly to ensure that they are not burning on the outside.

Serve these easy-to-prepare tortillas to friends or as a special family supper. The chicken filling has a mild, spicy heat. A fresh salad makes a perfect accompaniment.

Spicy Chicken Tortillas

SERVES 4

2 tbsp oil
8 skinless, boneless chicken thighs, sliced
1 onion, chopped
2 garlic cloves, chopped
1 tsp cumin seeds, crushed roughly
2 large dried chilies, sliced
14 oz/400 g canned tomatoes
14 oz/400 g canned red kidney beans, drained and rinsed
⅔ cup Fresh Chicken Bouillon (see page 14)
2 tsp sugar
salt and pepper

to serve

1 large ripe avocado, pitted
1 lime
8 soft tortillas
1 cup thick plain yogurt

1 Heat the oil in a large skillet, add the chicken and sauté for 3 minutes, until golden. Add the onion and sauté for 5 minutes, stirring until browned. Add the garlic, cumin, and chilies, with their seeds, and cook for about 1 minute.

2 Add the tomatoes, kidney beans, bouillon, and sugar, and season with salt and pepper to taste. Bring to a boil, breaking up the tomatoes. Reduce the heat, cover and simmer for 15 minutes. Remove the lid and cook for 5 minutes, stirring occasionally, until the sauce has thickened.

3 Mash the avocado with a fork. Cut half of the lime into 8 thin wedges. Squeeze the juice from the remaining lime over the avocado.

4 Warm the tortillas, according to the package directions. Put 2 tortillas on each serving plate, fill with the chicken mixture and top with spoonfuls of avocado and yogurt. Garnish the tortillas with lime wedges.

NUTRITION

Calories *650*; Sugars *15 g*; Protein *48 g*; Carbohydrate *47 g*; Fat *31 g*; Saturates *10 g*

easy
10 mins
35 mins

COOK'S TIP

If serving these to children, or you want an even milder flavor either remove the seeds from the chilies before using, or omit the chilies altogether.

A tasty alternative to traditional hamburgers, these lamb burgers are flavored with mint jelly and accompanied with a smooth minty dressing.

Minty Lamb Burgers

1 Place the lamb in a large bowl and mix in the onion, bread crumbs, and mint jelly. Season with salt and pepper to taste, then mold the ingredients together with your hands to form a firm mixture.

2 Divide the mixture into 4 and shape each portion into a round, measuring 4-inches/10-cm in diameter. Place the rounds on a plate lined with baking parchment and leave to chill for 30 minutes.

3 Preheat the broiler to medium. Line a broiler rack with baking parchment, securing the ends under the rack, and place the burgers on top. Broil for 8 minutes, then turn over the burgers and cook for another 7 minutes, or until cooked through.

4 Meanwhile, make the relish. In a small bowl, mix together the plain yogurt, mint jelly, cucumber and fresh mint. Cover the relish with plastic wrap and let chill in the refrigerator for 1 hour, or until required.

5 Drain the burgers on paper towels. Serve the burgers inside the baps with sliced tomatoes, cucumber, lettuce, and relish.

SERVES 4

350 g/12 oz ground lean lamb,
1 onion, chopped finely
4 tbsp dry whole-wheat bread crumbs
2 tbsp mint jelly
salt and pepper

to serve

4 whole-wheat baps, split
2 large tomatoes, sliced
small piece of cucumber, sliced
lettuce leaves

relish

4 tbsp low-fat plain yogurt or fromage frais
1 tbsp mint jelly, softened
2-inch/5-cm piece of cucumber, diced finely
1 tbsp chopped fresh mint

NUTRITION

Calories *320*; Sugars *11 g*; Protein *28 g*; Carbohydrate *33 g*; Fat *10 g*; Saturates *4 g*

 moderate

1 hr

15 mins

These little meatballs, served with a minty yogurt dressing, can be prepared well in advance, ready to cook when required.

Lamb *and* Tomato Koftas

SERVES 4

8 oz/225 g finely ground lean lamb
1½ onions
1–2 garlic cloves, crushed
1 dried red chili, chopped finely (optional)
2–3 tsp garam masala
2 tbsp chopped fresh mint
2 tsp lemon juice
salt
2 tbsp vegetable oil
4 small tomatoes, quartered
sprigs of fresh mint, to garnish

yogurt dressing
⅔ cup low-fat plain yogurt
2-inch/5-cm piece of cucumber, grated
2 tbsp chopped fresh mint
½ tsp toasted cumin seeds (optional)

1 Place the lamb in a bowl. Finely chop 1 onion and add to the bowl with the garlic and chili, if using. Stir in the garam masala, mint, and lemon juice, and season with salt to taste. Mix well.

2 Divide the mixture in half, then divide each half into 10 equal portions and form each into a small ball. Roll the balls in the oil to coat. Cut the remaining onion half into fourths and separate into layers.

3 Thread 5 of the spicy meatballs, alternating with the tomato pieces, and some of the onion layers onto each of 4 pre-soaked wooden or metal skewers.

4 Brush the vegetables with the remaining oil and cook the koftas under a preheated hot broiler for about 10 minutes, turning frequently, until they are browned all over and cooked through.

5 Meanwhile, prepare the yogurt dressing for the koftas. In a small bowl, mix together the yogurt, cucumber, mint, and cumin seeds, if using.

6 Garnish the lamb and tomato koftas with mint sprigs and place on a large serving platter. Serve the koftas hot with the yogurt dressing.

NUTRITION
Calories *183*; Sugars *5 g*; Protein *15 g*; Carbohydrate *5 g*; Fat *11 g*; Saturates *4 g*

easy

15 mins

10 mins

Lean ham wrapped around crisp celery, topped with a light crust of cheese and scallions, makes a delicious light lunch.

Cheese *and* Ham Savory

1 Lay the slices of ham on a cutting board. Place a piece of celery on each piece of ham and roll up. Place 3 ham and celery rolls in each of 4 small, heatproof dishes.

2 Sprinkle the scallions over the ham and celery rolls and season with celery salt and pepper to taste.

3 Combine the soft cheese and yogurt and spoon the mixture over the ham and celery rolls.

4 Preheat the broiler to medium. Sprinkle each portion with 1 tablespoon Parmesan cheese and broil for 6–7 minutes, until hot and the cheese has formed a crust. If the cheese starts to brown too quickly, lower the broiler setting slightly.

5 Garnish the ham and celery rolls with celery leaves and serve with a tomato salad and crusty bread.

SERVES 4

12 thin slices of lean ham
4 celery stalks, each cut into 3 pieces, the leaves reserved, to garnish
1 bunch of scallions, shredded finely
3/4 cup low-fat soft cheese with garlic and herbs
6 tbsp low-fat plain yogurt
4 tbsp freshly grated Parmesan cheese
celery salt and pepper

to serve
tomato salad
crusty bread

NUTRITION

Calories *140*; Sugars *3 g*; Protein *3 g*; Carbohydrate *20 g*; Fat *17 g*; Saturates *1 g*

 moderate
15 mins
 10 mins

COOK'S TIP

Parmesan is a good cheese to use in low-fat recipes because its intense flavor means you need to use only a small amount.

Meat

The growing awareness of the importance of healthy eating means that super stores and butchers now offer leaner, lower-fat cuts of meat. Although these are slightly more expensive than standard cuts, you do not need to buy as much if you combine them with lots of tasty vegetables and low-fat sauces. It is also worth spending a little extra time cooking the meat carefully to enhance its flavor. Always remember to cut any visible fat from beef and pork before you cook it. Liver, kidney, and venison are relatively low in fat. Look out for extra lean ground meats, which can be dry-fried without the addition of oil or fat.

Probably the best-known Mexican dish and a great favorite of many. The chili content can be increased to suit your taste.

Chili *con* Carne

SERVES 4

- 2 tbsp vegetable oil
- 1 lb 10 oz/750 g lean braising or stewing steak, cut into ¾-inch/2-cm cubes
- 1 large onion, sliced
- 2–4 garlic cloves, crushed
- 1 tbsp all-purpose flour
- scant 2 cups tomato juice
- 14 oz/400 g canned tomatoes
- 1–2 tbsp sweet chile sauce
- 1 tsp ground cumin
- 15 oz/425 g canned red kidney beans, drained and rinsed
- ½ teaspoon dried oregano
- 1–2 tbsp chopped fresh parsley
- salt and pepper
- chopped fresh herbs, to garnish

to serve

- plain rice
- tortillas

1 Heat the oil in a large, flameproof casserole and cook the beef until well seared. Remove the beef from the casserole.

2 Add the onion and garlic to the casserole and cook until lightly browned. Stir in the flour and cook for 1–2 minutes. Stir in the tomato juice and tomatoes and bring to a boil. Return the beef to the casserole with the chile sauce, ground cumin, and season with salt and pepper to taste. Cover and place in a preheated oven, 325°F/160°C, for 1½ hours, or until the beef is almost tender.

3 Stir in the beans, oregano, and parsley and adjust the seasoning. Cover the casserole and return to the oven for 45 minutes. Serve sprinkled with herbs with plain rice and tortillas.

NUTRITION

Calories *443*; Sugars *11 g*; Protein *48 g*; Carbohydrate *30 g*; Fat *15 g*; Saturates *4 g*

easy

10 mins

2 hrs 45 mins

COOK'S TIP

Chili con carne requires quite a lengthy cooking time, but you can save time and energy by preparing double the quantity you need and freezing half of it to serve on another occasion. Freeze for 3–4 weeks and thaw before use.

This is one of the best-known curries. Rogan Josh means "red curry," and is so-called because of the red chiles in the recipe.

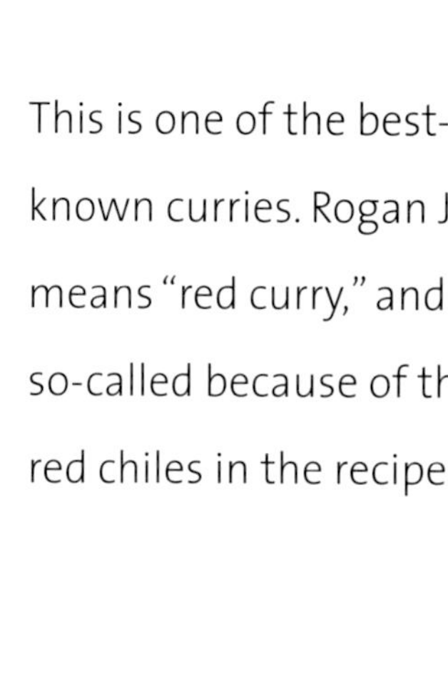

Rogan Josh

1 Heat the ghee in a large, flameproof casserole and brown the meat in batches. Remove the meat from the casserole and set aside in a bowl.

2 Add the onion to the ghee and cook over a high heat for 3–4 minutes, stirring occasionally.

3 In a bowl, grind together the garlic, ginger, chiles, cardamom, cloves, coriander seeds, cumin seeds, paprika, and salt. Add the spice paste and bay leaf to the casserole and stir until fragrant.

4 Return the meat and any juices in the bowl to the casserole and simmer for 2–3 minutes. Gradually stir the yogurt into the casserole, keeping the sauce simmering. Stir in the cinnamon stick and hot water, and pepper to taste.

5 Cover the casserole and cook in a preheated oven, 350°F/180°C, for 1¼ hours, until the meat is very tender and the sauce has slightly reduced. Discard the cinnamon stick and stir in the garam masala. Remove any oil from the surface of the casserole before serving.

SERVES 4

2 tbsp ghee
2 lb 4 oz/1 kg lean braising steak, cut into 1-inch/2.5-cm cubes
1 onion, chopped finely
3 garlic cloves
1-inch/2.5-cm piece of fresh gingerroot, grated
4 fresh red chiles, chopped
4 green cardamom pods
4 whole cloves
2 tsp coriander seeds
2 tsp cumin seeds
1 tsp paprika
1 tsp salt
1 bay leaf
¼ cup low-fat plain yogurt
1-inch/2.5-cm piece of cinnamon stick
⅔ cup hot water
¼ tsp garam masala
pepper

NUTRITION

Calories *248*; Sugars *2 g*; Protein *35 g*; Carbohydrate *2 g*; Fat *11 g*; Saturates *5 g*

 moderate

10 mins

1 hr 45 mins

Serve this old favorite with vegetables and herby dumplings for a substantial one-pot meal.

Boiled Beef *and* Carrots

SERVES 4

- about 3½ lb/1.75 kg joint salted silverside or topside
- 2 onions, quartered, or 5–8 small onions
- 8–10 whole cloves
- 2 bay leaves
- 1 cinnamon stick
- 2 tbsp brown sugar
- 4 large carrots, sliced thickly
- 1 turnip, quartered
- ½ swede, sliced thickly
- 1 large leek, sliced thickly
- 2 tbsp butter or margarine
- 4 tbsp all-purpose flour
- ½ tsp dried mustard powder
- salt and pepper

dumplings

- 2 cups self-rising flour
- ½ tsp dried sage
- ½ cup shredded vegetable suet
- about ⅔ cup water

NUTRITION

Calories *459*; Sugars *2 g*; Protein *31 g*; Carbohydrate *35 g*; Fat *22 g*; Saturates *10 g*

 challenging

 15 mins

 2 hrs 45 mins

1 Put the beef in a large pan, add the onions, cloves, bay leaves, cinnamon, sugar, and sufficient water to cover the meat. Bring slowly to a boil, removing any scum from the surface. Reduce the heat, cover and simmer gently for 1 hour.

2 Add the carrots, turnip, swede, and leek, cover and simmer for another 1¼ hours, until the beef is tender.

3 Meanwhile, make the dumplings. Strain the flour into a bowl, season well and mix in the herbs and suet. Add sufficient water to make a softish dough.

4 Divide the dough into 8 pieces, roughly shape into balls and place on top of the beef and vegetables. Replace the lid and simmer for 15–20 minutes.

5 Place the beef, vegetables and dumplings in a serving dish. Measure 1¼ cups of the cooking liquid into a pan. Blend the margarine with the flour, then gradually whisk into the pan and bring to a boil. Reduce the heat and simmer until thickened. Stir in the mustard, adjust the seasoning and serve with the beef.

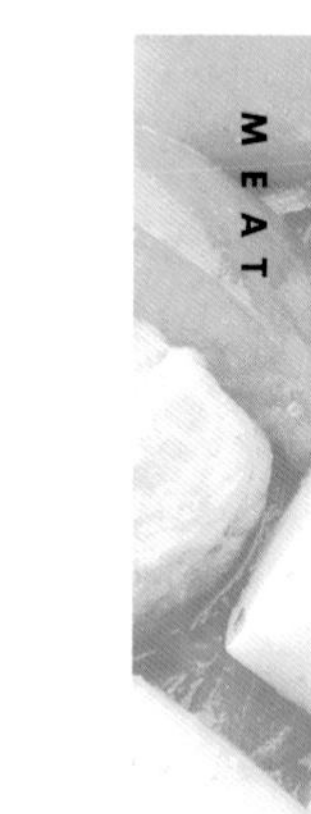

Ground lamb or beef is cooked here with onions, carrots, herbs, and tomatoes and with a delicious topping of piped creamed potatoes.

Shepherd's Pie

1 Place the meat in a heavy-based pan with no extra fat and cook gently, stirring frequently, until the meat begins to brown.

2 Add the onions, carrots, and garlic and continue to cook gently for about 10 minutes. Stir in the flour and cook for a minute or so, then gradually stir in the bouillon and tomatoes, then bring to a boil.

3 Reduce the heat, add the Worcestershire sauce and herbs, and season with salt and pepper to taste. Cover and simmer gently for about 25 minutes, stirring occasionally.

4 Cook the potatoes in boiling salted water until tender, then drain thoroughly and mash, beating in the butter, seasoning and sufficient milk to give a piping consistency. Place in a piping bag fitted with a large star tip.

5 Stir the mushrooms, if using, into the meat and adjust the seasoning. Turn into a shallow ovenproof dish.

6 Pipe the potatoes evenly over the meat. Cook in a preheated oven, 400°F/200°C, for about 30 minutes, until piping hot and the potatoes are golden brown.

COOK'S TIP

If liked, a mixture of boiled potatoes and parsnips or swede may be used for the topping.

SERVES 4

1 lb 9 oz/700 g lean ground lamb or beef
2 onions, chopped
8 oz/225 g carrots, diced
1–2 garlic cloves, crushed
1 tbsp all-purpose flour
scant 1 cup Fresh Beef Bouillon (see page 14)
7 oz/200 g canned chopped tomatoes
1 tsp Worcestershire sauce
1 tsp chopped fresh sage or oregano, or ½ tsp dried sage or oregano
1 lb 8 oz–2 lb/750 g–1 kg potatoes
2 tbsp butter or margarine
3–4 tbsp skim milk
1¾ cups sliced white mushrooms (optional)
salt and pepper

NUTRITION

Calories *378*; Sugars *8g*; Protein *33 g*; Carbohydrate *37 g*; Fat *12 g*; Saturates *4 g*

moderate

10 mins

1 hr 30 mins

Tenderloin, short loin, and round steak are all suitable cuts for this dish, although round steak retains the most flavor.

Steak *in a* Wine Marinade

SERVES 4

4 round steaks, about 9 oz/250 g each
2½ cups red wine
1 onion, quartered
2 tbsp Dijon mustard
2 garlic cloves, crushed
4 large portobello mushrooms
salt and pepper
olive oil, for brushing
fresh rosemary branch (optional)

1 Snip through the fat strip on the steaks in 3 places, so that the steak retains its shape when barbecue grilled.

2 Combine the red wine, onion, mustard, and garlic, and season with salt and pepper to taste. Lay the steaks in a shallow, nonmetallic dish and pour the marinade over. Cover and marinate in the refrigerator for 2–3 hours.

3 Remove the steaks from the refrigerator 30 minutes before you intend to cook them to let them come to room temperature. (This is especially important if the steak is thick, so that it cooks more evenly and is not well done on the outside and raw in the middle.)

4 Sear both sides of the steak—about 1 minute on each side—over a hot barbecue grill. If the steak is about 1-inch/2.5-cm thick, keep it over a hot barbecue and cook for about 4 minutes on each side. This will give a medium-rare steak—cook it more or less, to suit your taste. If the steak is a thicker cut, move it to a cooler part of the barbecue or farther away from the coals. To test the readiness of the meat while cooking, simply press it with your finger—the more the meat yields, the less it is cooked.

5 Brush the mushrooms with the olive oil and cook them alongside the steak for 5 minutes, turning once. At the same time, put the rosemary branch, if using, in the fire to flavor the meat slightly.

6 Remove the steak and set aside to rest for 1–2 minutes before serving. Slice the mushrooms and serve immediately with the meat.

NUTRITION

Calories *356*; Sugars *2 g*; Protein *41 g*; Carbohydrate *2 g*; Fat *9 g*; Saturates *4 g*

easy

2–3 hrs 10 mins

15 mins

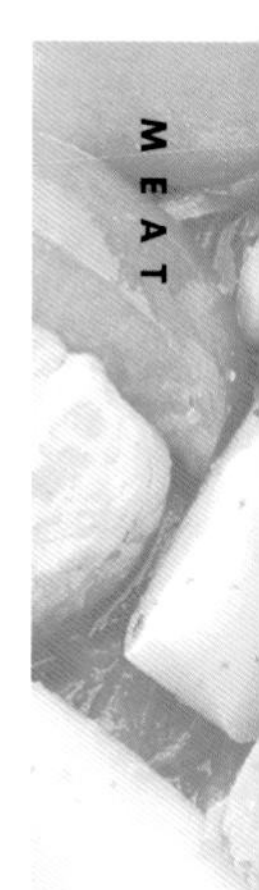

This Japanese-style teriyaki sauce complements grilled beef, but it can also be used to accompany chicken or salmon.

Beef Teriyaki

1 Place the meat in a shallow, nonmetallic dish. To make the sauce, combine the cornstarch with the sherry to make a smooth paste, then stir in the vinegar, soy sauce, sugar, garlic, cinnamon, and ginger. Pour the sauce over the meat, turn to coat, and set aside to marinate for at least 2 hours.

2 Remove the meat from the sauce, drain well, then pour it into a small pan.

3 Cut the meat into thin strips and thread these, concertina-style, onto 4–8 pre-soaked wooden skewers, alternating each strip of meat with pieces of scallion and yellow bell pepper.

4 Gently heat the sauce until it is just simmering, stirring occasionally.

5 Grill the kabobs over hot coals for 5–8 minutes, turning and basting the beef and vegetables occasionally with the reserved teriyaki sauce.

6 Arrange the skewers on serving plates and pour the remaining sauce over the kabobs. Serve immediately with salad greens.

SERVES 4

1 lb/450 g extra thin lean beef steaks
8 scallions, cut into short lengths
1 yellow bell pepper, halved, seeded, and cut into chunks
salad greens, to serve

sauce

1 tsp cornstarch
2 tbsp dry sherry
2 tbsp white wine vinegar
3 tbsp soy sauce
1 tbsp molasses sugar
1 garlic clove, crushed
½ tsp ground cinnamon
½ tsp ground ginger

NUTRITION

Calories *184*; Sugars *6 g*; Protein *24 g*; Carbohydrate *8 g*; Fat *5 g*; Saturates *2 g*

easy

2 hrs 15 mins

15 mins

Serve these fruity, hot and spicy steaks with noodles. Use a non-slip, ridged skillet to cook them to keep fat levels to a minimum.

Ginger Beef *with* Chili

SERVES 4

4 lean beef steaks, such as round, short loin or tenderloin, about 3½ oz/100 g each
2 tbsp ginger wine
1-inch/2.5-cm piece of fresh gingerroot, chopped finely
1 garlic clove, crushed
1 tsp ground chili
1 tsp vegetable oil
salt and pepper
fresh red chile strips, to garnish

to serve
freshly cooked noodles
2 scallions, shredded

relish
8 oz/225 g fresh pineapple, chopped
1 small red bell pepper, halved, seeded, and chopped finely
1 fresh red chile, seeded and chopped finely
2 tbsp light soy sauce
1 piece of preserved ginger in syrup, drained and chopped

NUTRITION
Calories *179*; Sugars *8 g*; Protein *21 g*; Carbohydrate *8 g*; Fat *6 g*; Saturates *2 g*

easy

40 mins
10 mins

1 Using a meat mallet or covered rolling pin, pound the steaks until they are ½-inch/1-cm thick. Season on both sides with salt and pepper to taste and place in a shallow, nonmetallic dish.

2 Combine the ginger wine, ginger, garlic, and chili and pour the mixture over the meat. Cover with plastic wrap and chill for 30 minutes.

3 Meanwhile, make the relish. Place the pineapple, red bell pepper, and red chile in a bowl. Add the soy sauce and preserved ginger and stir well. Cover with plastic wrap and chill until required.

4 Brush a ridged skillet with the oil and heat until very hot. Drain the beef and add to the skillet, pressing down to seal. Lower the heat and cook for 5 minutes. Turn the steaks over and cook for a further 5 minutes.

5 Drain the steaks on paper towels and transfer to warm serving plates. Garnish with chile strips and serve with noodles, scallions, and the relish.

COOK'S TIP

You can cook the steak for more or less time according to how you like your meat, cook longer if liked well done.

Lean pork chops, stuffed with an aniseed and orange filling, are pan-cooked with fennel in a sweet sauce.

Pork *with* Fennel *and* Aniseed

1 Using a small, sharp knife, make a slit in the center of each pork chop to create a pocket.

2 Mix the rice, orange peel, scallions and aniseed together in a bowl. Season with salt and pepper to taste.

3 Spoon the rice mixture into the pocket of each pork chop, then press gently to seal.

4 Heat the oil in a skillet and cook the pork chops on each side for 2–3 minutes, until lightly browned.

5 Add the fennel and orange juice to the pan, then bring to a boil. Reduce the heat and simmer for 15–20 minutes, until the meat is tender and cooked through. Remove the pork and fennel with a draining spoon and transfer to a serving plate.

6 Blend the cornstarch and Pernod together in a small bowl. Add the cornstarch mixture to the pan and stir it into the pan juices. Cook for 2–3 minutes, stirring, until the sauce has thickened.

7 Pour the Pernod sauce over the pork chops, garnish with fennel fronds and serve with broccoli flowerets.

SERVES 4

4 lean pork chops, about 4½ oz/125 g each, trimmed
⅓ cup cooked brown rice
1 tsp orange peel, grated
4 scallions, chopped finely
½ tsp aniseed
1 tbsp olive oil
1 fennel bulb, sliced thinly
2 cups unsweetened orange juice
1 tbsp cornstarch
2 tbsp Pernod
salt and pepper
fennel fronds, to garnish
broccoli florets, to serve

NUTRITION

Calories *298*; Sugars *10 g*; Protein *30 g*; Carbohydrate *18 g*; Fat *10 g*; Saturates *3 g*

moderate

20 mins

30 mins

In this traditional Chinese dish the pork turns "red" during cooking because it is basted in dark soy sauce.

Red Roast Pork *in* Soy Sauce

SERVES 4

1 lb/450 g lean pork tenderloin
6 tbsp dark soy sauce
2 tbsp dry sherry
1 tsp Chinese five-spice powder
2 garlic cloves, crushed
2 tsp chopped finely fresh gingerroot
1 large red bell pepper, halved, seeded, and cut into wedges
1 large yellow bell pepper, halved, seeded, and cut into wedges
1 large orange bell pepper, halved, seeded, and cut into wedges
4 tbsp superfine sugar
2 tbsp red wine vinegar

to garnish
scallions, shredded
snipped fresh chives

NUTRITION
Calories *268*; Sugars *20 g*; Protein *26 g*; Carbohydrate *22 g*; Fat *8 g*; Saturates *3 g*

moderate

1 hr 15 mins

1 hr 15 mins

1 Place the pork in a shallow, nonmetallic dish.

2 Mix together the soy sauce, sherry, Chinese five-spice powder, garlic, and ginger. Spoon the mixture over the pork, cover, and marinate in the refrigerator for at least 1 hour, or until required.

3 Drain the pork, reserving the marinade. Place the pork on a roasting rack over a roasting pan. Cook in a preheated oven, 375°F/190°C, occasionally basting with the marinade, for 1 hour, or until cooked through.

4 Arrange the red, yellow and orange bell peppers on a cookie sheet and bake alongside the pork for the last 30 minutes of cooking time.

5 Place the superfine sugar and vinegar in a pan and heat gently until the sugar dissolves. Bring to a boil, then reduce the heat and simmer for 3–4 minutes, until syrupy.

6 When the pork is cooked, remove it from the oven and brush with the sugar syrup. Let stand for about 5 minutes, then slice, and arrange on a warm serving plate.

7 Serve garnished with the scallions and fresh chives.

Tender, lean pork is cooked in a tasty, rich tomato sauce, and flavored with a tangy plain yogurt.

Pork Stroganoff

1 Heat the oil in a large pan. Add the pork, onion, and garlic and cook over low heat, stirring occasionally, for 4–5 minutes, until lightly browned.

2 Add the flour and tomato paste, pour in the bouillon, and stir to mix.

3 Add the mushrooms, green bell pepper, and nutmeg, and season with salt and pepper to taste. Bring to a boil, cover, and simmer for 20 minutes, until the pork is tender and cooked through.

4 Remove the pan from the heat, set aside to cool slightly, then stir in the yogurt.

5 Serve the pork and sauce on a bed of rice, with an extra spoonful of yogurt, and garnish with a dusting of ground nutmeg.

SERVES 4

1 tbsp vegetable oil
12 oz/350 g lean pork tenderloin, cut into ½-inch/1-cm thick slices
1 onion, chopped
2 garlic cloves, crushed
¼ cup all-purpose flour
2 tbsp tomato paste
2 cups Fresh Chicken or Fresh Vegetable Bouillon (see page 14)
1¾ cups sliced white mushrooms
1 large green bell pepper, seeded, and diced
½ tsp ground nutmeg, plus extra to garnish
4 tbsp low-fat plain yogurt, plus extra to serve
salt and pepper
cooked plain rice, to serve

NUTRITION

Calories *223*; Sugars *7 g*; Protein *22 g*; Carbohydrate *12 g*; Fat *10 g*; Saturates *3 g*

easy

 2 hrs 15 mins

 30 mins

COOK'S TIP

You can buy ready-made fresh bouillon from leading super store. Although expensive, they are more nutritious than bouillon cubes, which are high in salt and artificial flavorings.

These pork and apple kabobs are served with a mustard sauce, making an ideal light lunch.

Pork *and* Apple Skewers

SERVES 4

2 dessert apples, cored and cut into wedges
a little lemon juice
1 lb/450 g pork tenderloin, cut into bite-size pieces
1 lemon, sliced
2 tsp wholegrain mustard
2 tsp Dijon mustard
2 tbsp apple or orange juice
2 tbsp sunflower oil
crusty brown bread, to serve

mustard sauce
1 tbsp wholegrain mustard
1 tsp Dijon mustard
6 tbsp light cream

1 To make the mustard sauce, combine the wholegrain and Dijon mustards in a small bowl and slowly blend in the cream. Let stand until required.

2 Toss the apple wedges in the lemon juice to prevent any discoloration.

3 Thread the pork, apple, and lemon slices alternately on to 4 metal or pre-soaked wooden skewers.

4 Mix together the wholegrain and Dijon mustards, apple juice, and sunflower oil. Brush the mixture over the kabobs and grill over hot coals for 10–15 minutes, until cooked through, frequently turning and basting the kabobs with the mustard marinade.

5 Transfer the kabobs to warm serving plates and spoon a little of the mustard sauce over. Serve the kabobs with fresh, crusty brown bread.

NUTRITION
Calories *290*; Sugars *11 g*; Protein *24 g*; Carbohydrate *11 g*; Fat *17 g*; Saturates *5 g*

easy
 10 mins
 15 mins

These tasty pork fillets are broiled until tender in a parcel of foil, then served with a tangy orange sauce.

Tangy Pork Tenderloin

1 Place a large piece of double thickness foil in a shallow dish. Put the pork tenderloin in the center of the foil and season with salt and pepper to taste.

2 Heat the marmalade, orange peel and juice, vinegar, and Tabasco sauce in a small pan, stirring until the marmalade melts and the ingredients combine. Pour the mixture over the pork and wrap the meat in the foil. Seal the parcel well so that the juices cannot run out. Place over hot coals and broil for about 25 minutes, turning the parcel occasionally.

3 For the sauce, heat the oil and cook the onion for 2–3 minutes. Add the green bell pepper and cook for 3–4 minutes.

4 Remove the pork from the foil and place onto the rack. Pour the juices from the meat into the pan with the sauce.

5 Continue grilling the pork for another 10–20 minutes, turning, until cooked through and golden.

6 In a bowl, mix the cornstarch into a paste with the orange juice. Add to the sauce and cook, stirring, until the sauce has thickened. Slice the pork, spoon the sauce over, and serve with rice and mixed salad greens.

SERVES 4

14 oz/400 g lean pork tenderloin
3 tbsp orange marmalade
grated peel and juice of 1 orange
1 tbsp white wine vinegar
dash of Tabasco sauce
salt and pepper

sauce

1 tbsp olive oil
1 small onion, chopped
1 small green bell pepper, halved, seeded, and sliced thinly
1 tbsp cornstarch
$^{2}/_{3}$ cup orange juice

to serve

cooked plain rice
mixed salad greens

NUTRITION

Calories *230*; Sugars *16 g*; Protein *19 g*; Carbohydrate *20 g*; Fat *9 g*; Saturates *3 g*

easy

10 mins

55 mins

In this dish, the lean and tender cuts of meat are perfectly complemented by the sweet dessert apples and dry hard cider.

Pan-Cooked Pork Medallions

SERVES 4

8 lean pork medallions, about $1^3/_4$ oz/50 g each
2 tsp vegetable oil
1 onion, sliced finely
1 tsp superfine sugar
1 tsp dried sage
$^2/_3$ cup dry hard cider
$^2/_3$ cup Fresh Chicken or Vegetable Bouillon (see page 14)
1 green-skinned dessert apple, cored and cut into 8 wedges
1 red-skinned dessert apple, cored and cut into 8 wedges
1 tbsp lemon juice
salt and pepper
fresh sage leaves, to garnish

1 Discard the string from the pork and trim away any excess fat. Re-tie with clean string and set aside until required.

2 Heat the oil in a large skillet and gently cook the onion for about 5 minutes, until softened. Add the superfine sugar and cook for 3–4 minutes, until golden. Add the pork to the pan and cook for 2 minutes on each side, until browned.

3 Add the sage, hard cider and bouillon, then bring to a boil. Reduce the heat and simmer for 20 minutes.

4 Meanwhile, toss the apple wedges in lemon juice so that they do not turn brown when exposed to the air.

5 Add the apples to the pork and mix gently. Season with salt and pepper to taste and cook for another 3–4 minutes, until tender.

6 Remove the string from the pork and serve immediately, garnished with fresh sage leaves.

NUTRITION

Calories *256*; Sugars *12 g*; Protein *21 g*; Carbohydrate *12 g*; Fat *13 g*; Saturates *3 g*

easy

 20 mins

 40 mins

COOK'S TIP

Adding lemon juice to the cut apples pevents them from discoloring, making the end dish more attractive.

This is a pretty dish of pink tender lamb tenderloin served on a bed of light green mashed leeks and potatoes.

Lamb *with* Rosemary

1 Put the lamb in a shallow baking pan. Blend 2 tablespoons of the redcurrant jelly with the rosemary, garlic, and seasoning. Brush the mixture over the lamb and cook in a preheated oven, 450°F/230°C, brushing occasionally with any cooking juices, for 30 minutes.

2 Meanwhile, place the potatoes in a pan and cover with water. Bring to a boil, and cook for 8 minutes, until tender. Drain well.

3 Put the leeks in a pan with the bouillon, then bring to a boil. Reduce the heat, cover and simmer for 7–8 minutes, or until softened. Drain, reserving the cooking liquid.

4 Place the potato and leeks in a bowl and mash with a potato masher. Season with salt and pepper to taste and stir in the yogurt. Transfer to a warm platter and keep warm.

5 In a pan, melt the remaining redcurrant jelly and stir in the leek cooking liquid. Boil for 5 minutes.

6 Slice the lamb and arrange it over the mash. Spoon the sauce over the top. Garnish the lamb with rosemary and redcurrants and serve with steamed carrots.

SERVES 4

1 lb 2 oz/500 g lean lamb tenderloin
4 tbsp redcurrant jelly
1 tbsp chopped fresh rosemary
1 garlic clove, crushed
1 lb/450 g potatoes, diced
1 lb/450 g leeks, sliced
2/3 cup Fresh Vegetable Bouillon, (see page 14)
4 tsp low-fat plain yogurt or fromage frais
salt and pepper
steamed carrots, to serve

to garnish

chopped fresh rosemary
redcurrants

NUTRITION

Calories *388*; Sugars *11 g*; Protein *35 g*; Carbohydrate *38 g*; Fat *12 g*; Saturates *5 g*

moderate

15 mins

55 mins

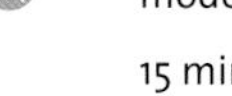

This classic recipe using lamb cutlets layered between sliced potatoes, kidneys, onions, and herbs, makes a perfect meal on a cold winter's day.

Lamb Hotpot

SERVES 4

- 1 lb 8 oz/675 g waxy potatoes, scrubbed and thinly sliced
- 1 lb 8 oz/675 g lean lamb shoulder chops
- 2 lambs' kidneys, prepared and sliced
- 1 large onion, sliced thinly
- 2 tbsp chopped fresh thyme
- ⅔ cup lamb bouillon
- 2 tbsp butter, melted
- salt and pepper
- fresh thyme sprigs, to garnish

1 Arrange a layer of potatoes in the bottom of a 3½ cup/1.7 liter ovenproof dish.

2 Arrange the lamb shoulder chops on top of the potatoes and cover with the kidneys, onion, and thyme.

3 Pour the lamb bouillon over the meat and then season to taste with salt and pepper.

4 Layer the remaining potato slices on top, overlapping to completely cover the meat and onion.

5 Brush the potato slices with the melted butter. Cover the dish, and cook in a preheated oven, 350°F/180°C, for 1½ hours.

6 Remove the lid and cook for another 30 minutes, until golden brown on top.

7 Garnish with fresh thyme sprigs and serve hot.

NUTRITION

Calories *420*; Sugars *2 g*; Protein *41 g*; Carbohydrate *31 g*; Fat *15 g*; Saturates *8 g*

 easy

 15 mins

 2 hrs

COOK'S TIP

Traditionally, oysters are also included in this tasty hotpot. Add them to the layers along with the kidneys, if wished.

Oranges and lamb are a great combination because the citrus flavor offsets the richer, fuller flavor of the meat.

Stir-Fried Lamb *with* Orange

1 Heat a wok or large, heavy-based skillet, without adding any oil.

2 Add the ground lamb to the wok. Dry-cook the ground lamb for 5 minutes, or until the meat is evenly browned. Drain away any excess fat from the wok.

3 Add the garlic, cumin seeds, ground coriander, and red onion to the wok and cook for a further 5 minutes.

4 Stir in the finely grated orange peel and juice, and the soy sauce, mixing until thoroughly combined. Cover, reduce the heat, and let simmer, stirring occasionally, for 15 minutes.

5 Remove the lid, increase the heat, and add the orange segments. Stir to mix.

6 Season with salt and pepper to taste and heat through for another 2–3 minutes.

7 Transfer the stir-fry to warm serving plates and garnish with fresh chives. Serve immediately.

SERVES 4

1 lb/450 g ground lamb
2 garlic cloves, crushed
1 tsp cumin seeds
1 tsp ground coriander
1 red onion, sliced
finely grated peel and juice of 1 orange
2 tbsp soy sauce
1 orange, peeled and segmented
salt and pepper
snipped fresh chives, to garnish

COOK'S TIP

If you wish to serve wine with your meal, try light, dry white wines and lighter Burgundy-style red wines as they blend well with spiced food.

NUTRITION

Calories *209*; Sugars *4 g*; Protein *25 g*; Carbohydrate *5 g*; Fat *10 g*; Saturates *5 g*

 easy

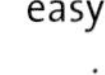 5 mins

  30 mins

These spicy lamb kabobs go well with the cool cucumber and yogurt dip. In fine weather, the kabobs can be barbecue grilled.

Minty Lamb Kabobs

SERVES 4

2 tsp coriander seeds
2 tsp cumin seeds
3 whole cloves
3 green cardamom pods
6 black peppercorns
½-inch/1-cm piece of fresh gingerroot
2 garlic cloves
2 tbsp chopped fresh mint
1 small onion, chopped
14 oz/400 g ground lamb
½ tsp salt
lime slices, to serve
fresh mint sprigs, to garnish

dip

½ cup low-fat plain yogurt
2 tbsp chopped fresh mint
3-inch/7-cm piece of cucumber, grated
1 tsp mango chutney

NUTRITION

Calories *295*; Sugars *4 g*; Protein *29 g*; Carbohydrate *4 g*; Fat *18 g*; Saturates *9 g*

easy

5 mins

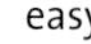

20 mins

1 Heat a skillet and dry-fry the coriander seeds, cumin seeds, cloves, cardamom pods, and peppercorns, until they turn a shade darker and release a roasted aroma.

2 Grind the spices in a coffee grinder, spice mill, or pestle and mortar.

3 Put the ginger and garlic into a food processor or blender and process to a purée. Add the ground spices, mint, onion, lamb, and salt and process until finely chopped. (Alternatively, finely chop the garlic and ginger and mix with the ground spices and remaining kebab ingredients.)

4 Mold the kebab mixture into small sausage shapes on 4 metal or pre-soaked wooden skewers. Cook under a preheated hot broiler for 10–15 minutes, turning the skewers occasionally.

5 To make the dip, mix together the yogurt, mint, cucumber, and mango chutney in a small bowl.

6 Serve the kabobs with lime slices and the cucumber and yogurt dip, and garnish with fresh mint sprigs.

COOK'S TIP

When dry-frying spices, watch them closely and move them around in the skillet continuously, as they can turn bitter very quickly.

Ground lamb makes a very tasty and authentic moussaka. For a change, use ground beef instead.

Lamb *and* Potato Moussaka

1 Lay the eggplant slices on a clean counter, or in a colander, and sprinkle liberally with salt, to extract the bitter juices. Leave for 10 minutes, then turn the slices over and repeat. Rinse and drain well.

2 Meanwhile, heat the oil in a pan and cook the onion and garlic for 3–4 minutes. Add the lamb and mushrooms and cook for 5 minutes, until browned. Stir in the tomatoes and bouillon, then bring to a boil. Reduce the heat and simmer for 10 minutes. Mix the cornstarch with the water and stir it into the pan, cook, stirring, until thickened.

3 Spoon half of the mixture into an ovenproof dish. Cover with the eggplant, then the remaining lamb mixture. Arrange the potatoes on top.

4 Beat together the eggs, soft cheese, and yogurt, and season with salt and pepper to taste. Pour the mixture over the potatoes to cover completely. Sprinkle with the cheese.

5 Bake in a preheated oven, 375°F/190°C, for 45 minutes, until the topping is set and golden brown. Garnish with flatleaf parsley and serve with mixed salad greens.

SERVES 4

1 large eggplant, sliced
1 tbsp olive or vegetable oil
1 onion, chopped finely
1 garlic clove, crushed
12 oz/350 g ground lean lamb
3½ cups sliced white mushrooms
15 oz/425 g canned chopped tomatoes with herbs
⅔ cup lamb or Fresh Vegetable Bouillon (see page 14)
2 tbsp cornstarch
2 tbsp water
1 lb 2 oz/500 g potatoes, par-boiled for 10 minutes and sliced
2 eggs
4½ oz/125 g low-fat soft cheese
½ cup low-fat plain yogurt
½ cup grated low-fat mature colby cheese
salt and pepper
fresh flatleaf parsley, to garnish
mixed salad greens, to serve

NUTRITION

Calories *422*; Sugars *8 g*; Protein *32 g*; Carbohydrate *35 g*; Fat *18 g*; Saturates *8 g*

 challenging

 30 mins

1 hr 5 mins

Dopiaza usually indicates a dish of meat cooked with plenty of onions; in this recipe the onions are cooked in two different ways.

Lamb Dopiaza

SERVES 4

- 2 tbsp ghee or vegetable oil
- 2 large onions, sliced finely
- 4 garlic cloves, 2 of them crushed
- 1 lb 10 oz/750 g lean boneless lamb, cut into 1-inch/2.5-cm cubes
- 1 tsp chili powder
- 1-inch/2.5-cm piece of fresh gingerroot, grated
- 2 fresh green chiles, chopped
- ½ tsp ground turmeric
- ½ cup low-fat plain yogurt
- 2 whole cloves
- 1-inch/2.5-cm cinnamon stick
- 1¼ cups water
- 2 tbsp chopped fresh cilantro
- 3 tbsp lemon juice
- salt and pepper
- naan bread, to serve

1 Heat the ghee in a large pan and add 1 onion and all the garlic, then cook for 2–3 minutes, stirring constantly.

2 Add the lamb and cook until browned all over. Remove and set aside. Add the chili powder, ginger, chiles, and turmeric to the pan and stir for another 30 seconds.

3 Add plenty of salt and pepper, the yogurt, cloves, cinnamon, and water.

4 Return the lamb to the pan, then bring to a boil. Reduce the heat and simmer for 10 minutes.

5 Transfer the mixture to an ovenproof dish and cook, uncovered, in a preheated oven, 350°F/180°C, for 40 minutes.

6 Adjust the seasoning, if necessary, stir in the remaining onion and cook, uncovered, for a further 40 minutes.

7 Add the fresh cilantro and lemon juice.

8 Transfer the lamb to a warm serving dish and serve with naan bread.

NUTRITION

Calories *433*; Sugars *6 g*; Protein *42 g*; Carbohydrate *7 g*; Fat *27 g*; Saturates *8 g*

moderate

10 mins

1 hr 35 mins

Rich game is best served with a sweet fruit sauce. Here, the venison steaks are cooked with juicy prunes and redcurrant jelly.

Venison *and* Garlic Mash

1 Season the venison with salt and pepper on both sides. Heat the oil in a heavy-based skillet and cook the venison with the onions for 2 minutes on each side until browned.

2 Reduce the heat and pour in the bouillon and wine. Add the redcurrant jelly and prunes and stir until the jelly melts. Cover and simmer for 10 minutes.

3 Meanwhile, make the garlic mash. Place the potatoes in a pan and cover with water. Bring to a boil and cook for 8–10 minutes, until tender. Drain well and mash until smooth. Add the garlic paste, yogurt, and parsley and blend thoroughly. Season, set aside, and keep warm.

4 Remove the medallions from the skillet with a draining spoon and keep warm.

5 Blend the cornstarch with the brandy in a small bowl and add to the pan juices. Heat, stirring, until thickened. Season with salt and pepper to taste. Serve the venison with the redcurrant and prune sauce, garlic mash and patty pans, if using.

COOK'S TIP

If you can not find garlic paste, simply cook garlic cloves with the potatoes and mash with the potatoes in step 3.

SERVES 4

8 medallions of venison, about 2¾ oz/75 g each
1 tbsp vegetable oil
1 red onion, chopped
⅔ cup Fresh Beef Bouillon (see page 15)
⅔ cup red wine
3 tbsp redcurrant jelly
3½ oz/100 g ready-to-eat dried, pitted prunes
2 tsp cornstarch
2 tbsp brandy
salt and pepper
patty pans, to serve (optional)

garlic mash

2 lb/900 g potatoes, diced
½ tsp garlic paste
2 tbsp low-fat plain yogurt or fromage frais
4 tbsp chopped fresh parsley

NUTRITION

Calories *602*; Sugars *18 g*; Protein *51 g*; Carbohydrate *62 g*; Fat *14 g*; Saturates *1 g*

 moderate

 10 mins

35 mins

Poultry

Chicken and turkey contain less fat than red meats, and even less if you remove the skin first. Duck is a rich meat with a distinctive flavor, and you only need a small amount to create flavorsome dishes which are healthy too. Since chicken does not have a very strong flavor, it marries well with other ingredients and the recipes in this chapter exploit that quality. Fruit features heavily in low-fat diets and it works particularly well with poultry. In this chapter, there are several examples: Roast Duck with Apple, Pot Roast Orange Chicken, and Lime Fricassée of Chicken. Broiling or barbecue grilling, is a very healthy way to cook as it requires little or no fat, and it produces deliciously succulent meat with a crispy coating, for example, Mediterranean Chicken.

Make sure the barbecue grill is really hot before you start cooking. The coals should be white and glow red when fanned.

Chicken *in* Spicy Yogurt

SERVES 4

3 dried red chilies
2 tbsp coriander seeds
2 tsp ground turmeric
2 tsp garam masala
4 garlic cloves, crushed
½ onion, chopped
1-inch/2.5-cm piece of fresh gingerroot, grated
2 tbsp lime juice
1 tsp salt
½ cup low-fat plain yogurt
1 tbsp oil
4 lb 8 oz/2 kg skinless chicken, cut into 6 pieces, or 6 chicken portions

to serve

tomatoes, chopped
cucumber, diced
red onion, sliced
raita dip

NUTRITION

Calories *74*; Sugars *2 g*; Protein *9 g*; Carbohydrate *2 g*; Fat *4 g*; Saturates *1 g*

 moderate

4 hrs 45 mins

25 mins

1 Grind together the chilies, coriander seeds, ground turmeric, garam masala, garlic, onion, ginger, lime juice, and salt in a pestle and mortar or grinder.

2 Gently heat a skillet and add the spice mixture. Stir until fragrant, about 2 minutes, and turn into a shallow, nonmetallic dish.

3 Add the yogurt and oil to the spice paste and mix well to combine.

4 Make 3 slashes in the flesh of each piece of chicken. Add the chicken to the dish containing the yogurt and spice mixture and coat the pieces completely in the marinade. Cover with plastic wrap and chill for at least 4 hours. Remove the dish from the refrigerator and leave covered at room temperature for 30 minutes before cooking.

5 Wrap the chicken pieces in foil, sealing well so the juices cannot escape.

6 Cook the chicken pieces over a very hot barbecue grill for about 15 minutes, turning once.

7 Remove the foil, with tongs, and brown the chicken on the grill for another 5 minutes.

8 Serve the chicken with the tomatoes, cucumber, red onion, and the raita dip

Traditionally, chicken tikka is cooked in a clay tandoori oven, but it works well on the barbecue grill, too.

Chicken Tikka

1 Place the chicken in a nonmetalic dish and sprinkle with the salt and the lemon juice. Set aside for 10 minutes.

2 To make the marinade, combine all the ingredients in a small bowl.

3 Thread the cubes of chicken onto pre-soaked wooden skewers. Brush the marinade over the chicken. Cover and set aside to marinate in the refrigerator for at least 2 hours, preferably overnight. Cook the chicken skewers on a barbecue grill over hot coals, brushing with oil and turning frequently, for 15 minutes, or until cooked through.

4 Meanwhile, combine the yogurt and mint sauce to make the dip and serve with the chicken.

SERVES 4

4 skinless, boneless chicken breast portions, cut into 1-inch/2.5-cm cubes
½ tsp salt
4 tbsp lemon or lime juice
vegetable oil, for brushing

marinade

⅔ cup low-fat plain yogurt
2 garlic cloves, crushed
1-inch/2.5-cm piece of fresh gingerroot grated
1 tsp ground cumin
1 tsp chili powder
½ tsp ground coriander
½ tsp ground turmeric

dip

⅔ cup low-fat plain yogurt
1 tsp mint jelly

NUTRITION

Calories *173*; Sugars *6 g*; Protein *28 g*; Carbohydrate *6 g*; Fat *4 g*; Saturates *2 g*

easy
2 hrs 15 mins–8 hrs
15 mins

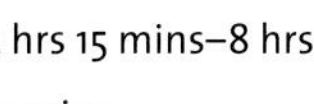

COOK'S TIP

Try pre-soaking the wooden skewers in water to prevent them from burning when cooking.

This is a really colorful dish, the red of the tomatoes perfectly complementing the orange sweet potato.

Thai Red Chicken

SERVES 4

1 tbsp sunflower oil
1 lb skinless, boneless chicken, sliced thinly
2 garlic cloves, chopped finely
2 tbsp Thai red curry paste
2 tbsp grated fresh galangal or gingerroot
1 tbsp tamarind paste
4 lime leaves
2½ cups coconut milk
8 oz/225 g sweet potato, diced
8 oz/225 g cherry tomatoes, halved
3 tbsp chopped fresh cilantro
cooked jasmine or Thai fragrant rice, to serve

1 Heat the sunflower oil in a preheated wok or large, heavy-based skillet.

2 Add the chicken to the wok and cook for 5 minutes.

3 Add the garlic, curry paste, galangal, tamarind, and lime leaves to the wok and cook for 1 minute.

4 Add the coconut milk and sweet potato to the mixture in the wok and bring to a boil. Allow to bubble over medium heat for 20 minutes, or until the juices start to thicken and reduce.

5 Add the cherry tomatoes and cilantro to the curry and cook for another 5 minutes, stirring occasionally. Transfer to serving plates and serve hot with jasmine rice.

NUTRITION
Calories *249*; Sugars *14 g*; Protein *26 g*; Carbohydrate *22 g*; Fat *7 g*; Saturates *2 g*

 easy
 15 mins
35 mins

COOK'S TIP

Galangal is very similar to gingerroot and is used in Thai cuisine. It can be bought fresh from Asian food stores, but is also available dry and as a powder. The fresh root needs to be peeled before use.

Chicken wings and corn coated in a sticky ginger marinade should be eaten with the fingers—there's no other way!

Ginger Chicken *and* Corn

1 Place the corn in a large bowl with the chicken wings.

2 Place the ginger in a bowl and add the lemon juice, sunflower oil, and golden superfine sugar. Mix together until thoroughly combined.

3 Toss the corn and chicken in the ginger mixture to coat evenly.

4 Thread the corn and chicken wings in alternate pieces onto metal or pre-soaked wooden skewers.

5 Cook under a preheated medium-hot broiler or on a barbecue grill for about 15–20 minutes, basting with the ginger glaze and turning frequently until the corn is golden brown and tender and the chicken is cooked. Serve immediately with baked potatoes and mixed salad greens.

SERVES 4

3 corn cobs, each cut into 6 pieces
12 chicken wings
1-inch/2.5-cm piece of fresh gingerroot, grated or chopped finely
6 tbsp lemon juice
4 tsp sunflower oil
1 tbsp golden superfine sugar

to serve
baked potatoes
mixed salad greens

COOK'S TIP

Cut off the wing tips before cooking because they burn very easily. Alternatively, you can cover them with small pieces of foil.

NUTRITION

Calories *123*; Sugars *3 g*; Protein *14 g*; Carbohydrate *3 g*; Fat *6 g*; Saturates *1 g*

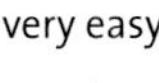

very easy
10 mins
20 mins

An attractive entrée of chicken breast portions filled with mixed bell peppers and set on a delicious tomato sauce.

Crispy Stuffed Chicken

SERVES 4

- 4 skinless, boneless chicken breast portions, about 5½ oz/150 g each
- 4 fresh tarragon sprigs
- ½ orange bell pepper, halved, seeded, and sliced
- ½ green bell pepper, halved, seeded, and sliced
- ½ cup whole-wheat bread crumbs
- 1 tbsp sesame seeds
- 4 tbsp lemon juice
- 1 small red bell pepper, halved and seeded
- 7 oz/200 g canned chopped tomatoes
- 1 small fresh red chile, seeded and chopped
- ¼ tsp celery salt
- salt and pepper
- fresh tarragon, to garnish

1 Make a slit in each of the chicken portions with a small, sharp knife to create a pocket. Season inside each pocket with salt and pepper.

2 Place a tarragon sprig and a few slices of orange and green bell pepper in each pocket. Place the chicken on a non-slip cookie sheet and sprinkle with the bread crumbs and sesame seeds.

3 Spoon 1 tablespoon of lemon juice over each chicken portion and bake in a preheated oven, 375°F/190°C, for 35–40 minutes, until the chicken is tender and cooked through.

4 Meanwhile, preheat the broiler to hot. Arrange the red bell pepper halves, skin-side up, on the rack and cook for 5–6 minutes, until the skin begins to char and blister. Set the broiled bell peppers aside to cool for about 10 minutes, then peel off the skins.

5 Put the red bell pepper in a blender, add the tomatoes, chile, and celery salt and process for a few seconds. Season to taste. (Alternatively, finely chop the red bell pepper and press through a strainer with the tomatoes and chile.)

6 When the chicken is cooked, heat the sauce, spoon a little onto a warm plate, and arrange a chicken in the center. Garnish with tarragon and serve.

NUTRITION

Calories *196*; Sugars *4 g*; Protein *29 g*; Carbohydrate *6 g*; Fat *6 g*; Saturates *2 g*

 challenging

 20 mins

50 mins

This sweet-citrus chicken is delicious hot or cold. Sesame-flavored noodles are the ideal accompaniment for the hot version.

Sweet *and* Sour Chicken

1 Using a sharp knife, score the chicken breast portions with a criss-cross pattern on both sides (making sure that you do not cut all the way through the meat.)

2 Combine the honey, soy sauce, lemon peel, and juice in a small bowl and season with black pepper.

3 Arrange the chicken on the broiler rack and brush with half the honey mixture. Cook under a preheated broiler for 10 minutes, then turn over and brush with the remaining mixture. Cook for a further 8–10 minutes, or until cooked through and tender. The juices should run clear when the thickest part of the chicken is pierced with a skewer.

4 Meanwhile, prepare the noodles, according to the package instructions. Drain well and transfer to a warm serving bowl. Add the sesame oil, sesame seeds, and lemon peel and toss well to mix. Season with salt and pepper to taste and keep warm.

5 Drain the chicken and serve immediately with a small mound of noodles, garnished with chives and lemon rind.

COOK'S TIP

These chicken breasts are also ideal for cooking on a barbecue grill, just ensure the flames have died down and the coals are hot.

SERVES 4

4 skinless, boneless chicken breast portions, about $4\frac{1}{2}$ oz/125 g each
2 tbsp honey
1 tbsp dark soy sauce
1 tsp finely grated lemon peel
1 tbsp lemon juice
salt and pepper

to garnish

1 tbsp chopped fresh chives
grated lemon rind

to serve

8 oz/225 g rice noodles
2 tsp sesame oil
1 tbsp sesame seeds
1 tsp finely grated lemon peel

NUTRITION

Calories *248*; Sugars *8 g*; Protein *30 g*; Carbohydrate *16 g*; Fat *8 g*; Saturates *2 g*

easy

5 mins

25 mins

Poussins are ideal for a one or two portion meal, and can be cooked very easily and quickly for a special dinner. If you're cooking for one, a microwave makes it even more convenient.

Poussin *with* Dried Fruits

SERVES 4

3/4 cup dried apples, peaches, and prunes
1/2 cup boiling water
2 poussins
1/3 cup walnut halves
1 tbsp honey
1 tsp ground allspice
1 tbsp walnut oil
salt and pepper

to serve
fresh vegetables
new potatoes

1 Place the dried fruits in a bowl, cover with the boiling water, and leave to stand for about 30 minutes.

2 Cut the poussins in half down the breastbone using a sharp knife, or leave them whole, if preferred.

3 Mix the fruit and any juices remaining in the bowl with the walnut halves, honey, and ground allspice and divide the mixture between 2 roasting bags or squares of foil, large enough to wrap the chickens.

4 Brush the poussins with walnut oil and season with salt and pepper to taste, then place on top of the fruits.

5 Close the roasting bags or fold the foil over to enclose the poussins and bake on a cookie sheet in a preheated oven, 375°F/190°C, for 25–30 minutes, or until the juices run clear and not pink when the poussin is pierced in the thickest part with a skewer. (To cook in a microwave, use microwave roasting bags and cook on High power for 6–7 minutes.)

6 Serve hot with fresh vegetables and new potatoes.

NUTRITION
Calories *316*; Sugars *23 g*; Protein *23 g*; Carbohydrate *23 g*; Fat *15 g*; Saturates *2 g*

 easy
 35 mins
 30 mins

COOK'S TIP

Alternative dried fruits that can be used in this recipe are cherries, mangoes, and/or papaya.

This colorful, nutritious pot-roast could be served for a family meal or for a special dinner. Add more vegetables if you're feeding a crowd—if your roasting pot is large enough!

Pot-Roast Orange Chicken

1 Heat the oil in a large, flameproof casserole and sauté the chicken, turning occasionally until evenly browned.

2 Cut one orange in half and place half inside the chicken cavity. Place the chicken in the casserole. Arrange the onions and carrots around the chicken.

3 Pour the orange juice over the chicken and season with salt and pepper to taste. Cut the remaining oranges into thin wedges and tuck around the chicken in the casserole, among the vegetables.

4 Cover and cook in a preheated oven, 350°F/180°C, for about 1½ hours, or until there is no trace of pink in the juices when the thickest part of the chicken is pierced with a skewer, and the vegetables are tender. Remove the lid and sprinkle with the brandy and sesame seeds, and return to the oven for 10 minutes.

5 To serve, lift the chicken on to a large platter. Place the vegetables around the chicken. Skim any excess fat from the juices. Blend the cornstarch with the water, stir it into the juices, and bring to a boil, stirring all the time. Adjust the seasoning to taste, then serve the sauce with the chicken.

SERVES 4

2 tbsp sunflower oil
1 chicken, weighing about 3 lb 5 oz
2 large oranges
2 small onions, cut into fourth
2 cups small whole carrots or thin carrots, cut into 2-inch/5-cm pieces
⅔ cup orange juice
2 tbsp brandy
2 tbsp sesame seeds
1 tbsp cornstarch mixed with 1 tbsp water
salt and pepper

NUTRITION

Calories *302*; Sugars *17 g*; Protein *29 g*; Carbohydrate *22 g*; Fat *11 g*; Saturates *2 g*

challenging

10 mins

2 hrs

This recipe uses ingredients found in the Languedoc area of France, where cooking over hot embers is a way of life.

Mediterranean Chicken

SERVES 4

4 tbsp low-fat plain yogurt
3 tbsp sun-dried tomato paste
1 tbsp olive oil
¼ cup lightly crushed fresh basil leaves
2 garlic cloves, chopped roughly
4 chicken quarters
salad greens, to serve

1 Combine the yogurt, tomato paste, olive oil, basil leaves, and garlic in a small bowl and stir well to mix.

2 Put the marinade into a dish large enough to hold the chicken quarters in a single layer. Add the chicken quarters. Make sure that the chicken pieces are thoroughly coated in the marinade.

3 Leave to marinate in the refrigerator for 2 hours. Remove and leave covered at room temperature for 30 minutes.

4 Place the chicken over a medium–hot barbecue grill and cook for 30–40 minutes, turning frequently, until the juices run clear when the thickest part of the chicken is pierced with a skewer.

5 Serve hot with a green salad. (It is also delicious eaten cold.)

NUTRITION

Calories *143*; Sugars *4 g*; Protein *13 g*; Carbohydrate *4 g*; Fat *8 g*; Saturates *2 g*

 easy
2 hrs 45 mins
30 mins

COOK'S TIP

For a marinade with an extra zingy flavor combine 2 garlic cloves, coarsely chopped, the juice of 2 lemons, and 3 tablespoons of olive oil, and cook in the same way.

With its red and yellow bell pepper sauces, this quick and simple dish is colorful, healthy, and perfect for an impromptu lunch or light supper.

Chicken *with* Two Sauces

1 Heat 1 tablespoon of the olive oil in each of 2 separate medium pans. Place half the onion, 1 garlic clove, the red bell peppers, cayenne pepper, and tomato paste in one pan. Place the remaining onion and garlic, the yellow bell peppers, and basil in the other pan.

2 Cover each pan and cook over very low heat for 1 hour, until the bell peppers are very soft. If either mixture becomes dry, add a little water. Transfer the contents of the first pan to a food processor and process, then strain. Repeat with the contents of the other pan.

3 Return the sauces to the separate pans and season with salt and pepper to taste. Gently reheat the sauces while the chicken is cooking.

4 Put the chicken portions into a skillet and add the wine and bouillon. Add the bouquet garni and bring to a boil. Reduce the heat, then simmer over a medium–low heat. Cook the chicken for about 20 minutes, until tender and cooked through.

5 To serve, put a pool of each sauce onto 4 individual serving plates, slice the chicken breast portions and arrange them on top. Garnish with fresh herbs and serve immediately.

SERVES 4

2 tbsp olive oil
2 onions, chopped finely
2 garlic cloves, crushed
2 red bell peppers, halved, seeded, and chopped
pinch of cayenne pepper
2 tsp tomato paste
2 yellow bell peppers, halved, seeded, and chopped
pinch of dried basil
4 skinless, boneless chicken breast portions
⅔ cup dry white wine
⅔ cup Fresh Chicken Bouillon (see page 14)
1 Fresh Bouquet Garni (see page 15)
salt and pepper
fresh herbs, to garnish

NUTRITION

Calories *257*; Sugars *7 g*; Protein *29 g*; Carbohydrate *8 g*; Fat *10 g*; Saturates *2 g*

 moderate

10 mins

1 hr 30 mins

Here, chicken breasts are served with a velvety sauce made from whiskey and plain yogurt.

Chicken *with* Whiskey Sauce

SERVES 4

2 tbsp butter
½ cup shredded leeks
⅓ cup diced carrots
¼ cup diced celery stalks
4 shallots, sliced
2½ cups Fresh Chicken Bouillon (see page 14)
6 skinless, boneless chicken breasts
¼ cup whiskey
1 scant cup low-fat plain yogurt
2 tbsp freshly grated horseradish
1 tsp honey, warmed
1 tsp chopped fresh parsley
salt and pepper
fresh parsley sprigs, to garnish

to serve
vegetable patty
mashed potato
fresh vegetables

1 Melt the butter in a large pan and add the leeks, carrots, celery, and shallots. Cook for 3 minutes, add half the chicken bouillon, and cook for about 8 minutes.

2 Add the remaining chicken bouillon, bring to a boil, add the chicken breasts, and cook for 10 minutes.

3 Remove the chicken and thinly slice. Place on a large, hot serving dish and keep warm until required.

4 In another pan, heat the whiskey until reduced by half. Strain the chicken bouillon through a fine strainer, add to the pan, and cook until the liquid has reduced by half.

5 Add the yogurt, horseradish, and honey. Heat gently and add the parsley and season with salt and pepper to taste. Stir until well blended.

6 Pour a little of the whiskey sauce around the chicken and pour the remaining sauce into a sauceboat to serve.

7 Serve the chicken with a vegetable patty made from the leftover vegetables, mashed potato, and fresh vegetables. Garnish with the parsley sprigs.

NUTRITION
Calories *337*; Sugars *6 g*; Protein *37 g*; Carbohydrate *6 g*; Fat *15 g*; Saturates *8 g*

 easy
5 mins
30 mins

These need to be eaten with your fingers so they are perfect for an informal supper dish.

Sticky Chicken Wings

1 Heat the olive oil in a large skillet and cook the onion and garlic for about 10 minutes.

2 Add the crushed tomatoes, dried herbs, fennel seeds, red wine vinegar, mustard, and cinnamon to the skillet along with the sugar, chili flakes, and treacle, and season with salt and pepper to taste. Bring to a boil, then reduce the heat and simmer gently for about 15 minutes, until the sauce has reduced slightly .

3 Put the chicken wings in a large dish, and coat liberally with the sauce. Leave to marinate in the refrigerator for 3 hours, or as long as possible, turning the wings over often in the marinade.

4 Transfer the wings to a cookie sheet, and roast in a preheated oven, 425°F/220°C, for 10 minutes. Reduce the heat to 375°F/190°C and cook for 20 minutes, basting often.

5 Serve the chicken wings piping hot, garnished with celery stalks and cherry tomatoes.

COOK'S TIP

The longer the chicken is marinated for, the more succulent and flavorsome the dish. If you have time marinate overnight.

SERVES 4

2 tbsp olive oil
1 small onion, chopped finely
2 garlic cloves, crushed
¾ pint crushed tomatoes
2 tsp dried thyme
1 tsp dried oregano
pinch of fennel seeds
3 tbsp red wine vinegar
2 tbsp Dijon mustard
pinch of ground cinnamon
2 tbsp brown sugar
1 tsp dried chili flakes
2 tbsp black treacle
16 chicken wings
salt and pepper

to garnish
celery stalks
cherry tomatoes

NUTRITION

Calories *165*; Sugars *12 g*; Protein *14 g*; Carbohydrate *12 g*; Fat *7 g*; Saturates *1 g*

 easy

3 hrs 15 mins

1 hr

This is perhaps one of the best known Caribbean dishes. The "jerk" in the name refers to the hot spicy coating.

Jerk Chicken

SERVES 4

4 chicken portions
1 bunch scallions, trimmed
1–2 Scotch Bonnet chiles, seeded
1 garlic clove
2-inch/5-cm piece of fresh gingerroot, chopped roughly
½ tsp dried thyme
½ tsp paprika
¼ tsp ground allspice
pinch of ground cinnamon
pinch of ground cloves
4 tbsp white wine vinegar
3 tbsp light soy sauce
pepper

1. Place the chicken portions in a shallow, nonmetallic dish.
2. Place the scallions, chiles, garlic, gingerroot, thyme, paprika, allspice, cinnamon, cloves, wine vinegar, soy sauce, and pepper to taste in a food processor and process to make a smooth mixture.
3. Pour the spicy mixture over the chicken. Turn the chicken portions over so that they are well coated in the marinade. Transfer the chicken to the refrigerator and leave to marinate for up to 24 hours.
4. Remove the chicken from the marinade and grill over medium-hot coals for about 30 minutes, turning the chicken over and basting occasionally with any remaining marinade, until the chicken is cooked through.
5. Transfer the chicken portions to individual serving plates and serve at once.

NUTRITION
Calories *158*; Sugars *0.4 g*; Protein *29 g*; Carbohydrate *2 g*; Fat *4 g*; Saturates *1 g*

 easy
 24 hrs
 30 mins

The addition of lime juice and lime peel adds a delicious tangy flavor to this chicken stew.

Lime Fricassee *of* Chicken

1 Coat the chicken pieces in the seasoned flour. Heat the oil in a large skillet and cook the chicken for about 4 minutes, until browned all over.

2 Using a draining spoon, transfer the chicken to a large, deep casserole and sprinkle with the sliced onions. Keep warm until required.

3 Slowly sauté the bell peppers in the juices remaining in the skillet.

4 Add the chicken bouillon and lime peel and juice, and cook for another 5 minutes.

5 Add the chiles, oyster sauce, and Worcestershire sauce. Season with salt and pepper to taste.

6 Pour the bell peppers and juices over the chicken and onions. Cover the casserole with a lid or cooking foil.

7 Cook in the center of a preheated oven, 375°F/190°C, for 1½ hours, until the chicken is very tender, then serve.

SERVES 4

1 large chicken, cut into small portions
½ cup all-purpose flour, seasoned
2 tbsp oil
1 lb 2 oz/500 g baby onions or shallots, sliced
1 each green and red bell pepper, halved, seeded, and sliced thinly
⅔ cup Fresh Chicken Bouillon (see page 14)
peel and juice of 2 limes
2 fresh chiles, chopped
2 tbsp oyster sauce
1 tsp Worcestershire sauce
salt and pepper

COOK'S TIP

Try this casserole with a cheese biscuit topping. About 30 minutes before the end of cooking time, simply top with rounds of cheese biscuit pastry.

NUTRITION

Calories *140*; Sugars *3 g*; Protein *3 g*; Carbohydrate *20 g*; Fat *17 g*; Saturates *1 g*

 moderate

 15 mins

1 hr 45 mins

Chile, tomatoes, and corn are typical ingredients in a Mexican dish. This is a quick and easy meal to serve for unexpected guests.

Mexican Chicken

SERVES 4

2 tbsp oil
8 chicken drumsticks
1 onion, chopped finely
1 tsp chili powder
1 tsp ground coriander
15 oz/425 g canned chopped tomatoes
2 tbsp tomato paste
2/3 cup frozen corn
salt and pepper

to serve
plain rice
mixed bell pepper salad

1 Heat the oil in a large skillet, add the chicken drumsticks and cook over a medium heat until lightly browned. Remove the chicken drumsticks from the pan with a draining spoon and set aside until required.

2 Add the onion to the pan and cook for 3–4 minutes, until softened, then stir in the chili powder and ground coriander and cook for a few seconds, stirring briskly so the spices do not burn on the bottom of the pan. Add the tomatoes and the tomato paste, and stir well to incorporate.

3 Return the chicken drumsticks to the pan and simmer gently for 20 minutes, until the chicken is tender and thoroughly cooked. Add the corn and cook for another 3–4 minutes. Season with salt and pepper to taste.

4 Serve with rice and mixed bell pepper salad.

NUTRITION
Calories *207*; Sugars *8 g*; Protein *18 g*; Carbohydrate *13 g*; Fat *9 g*; Saturates *2 g*

 easy
 15 mins
35 mins

COOK'S TIP

Mexican dishes are not usually suitable for freezing because the strong flavors they contain, such as chile, intensify during freezing, and if left for too long, can result in an unpleasant, musty flavor.

These chicken wings are brushed with a simple barbecue glaze, which can be made in minutes, but will be enjoyed by all.

Grilled Chicken

1 Remove the skin from the chicken if you want to reduce the fat in the dish.

2 To make the barbecue glaze, place the tomato paste, brown fruity sauce, white wine vinegar, honey, oil, and garlic in a small bowl. Mix the ingredients together until they are thoroughly blended.

3 Brush the glaze over the chicken and grill over hot coals for 15–20 minutes. Turn the chicken portions over occasionally and baste frequently with the barbecue glaze.

4 If the chicken begins to blacken before it is cooked, raise the rack if possible or move the chicken to a cooler part of the barbecue grill to slow down the cooking.

5 Transfer the grilled chicken to warm serving plates and serve with fresh salad greens.

SERVES 4

8 chicken wings or 1 chicken, cut into 8 portions
3 tbsp tomato paste
3 tbsp brown fruity sauce
1 tbsp white wine vinegar
1 tbsp clear honey
1 tbsp olive oil
1 garlic clove, crushed (optional)
salad greens, to serve

COOK'S TIP

When poultry is cooked over a very hot barbecue grill, the heat immediately seals in all of the juices, leaving the meat succulent. For this reason make sure that the coals are hot enough before starting to grill.

NUTRITION

Calories *143*; Sugars *6 g*; Protein *14 g*; Carbohydrate *6 g*; Fat *7 g*; Saturates *1 g*

 easy

15 mins

20 mins

The richly flavored stuffing in this recipe is cooked under the breast skin of the chicken, so not only is all the flavor sealed in, but the chicken stays really moist and succulent during cooking.

Festive Apple Chicken

SERVES 4

1 chicken, weighing about 4 lb 8 oz/2 kg
oil, for brushing
1 tbsp butter
2 dessert apples, cored and sliced
1 tbsp redcurrant jelly
mixed vegetables, to serve

stuffing

1 tbsp butter
1 small onion, chopped finely
2 oz/55 g mushrooms, chopped finely
2 oz/55 g smoked ham, chopped finely
½ cup fresh bread crumbs
1 tbsp chopped fresh parsley
1 crisp dessert apple, cored and grated coarsely
1 tbsp lemon juice
salt and pepper

1 To make the stuffing, melt the butter in a pan and sauté the onion gently, stirring, until softened, but not browned. Stir in the mushrooms and cook for 2–3 minutes. Remove from the heat and stir in the ham, bread crumbs, and the parsley.

2 Combine the stuffing mixture with the grated apple and lemon juice. Season with salt and pepper to taste.

3 Loosen the breast skin of the chicken and carefully spoon the stuffing mixture under it, smoothing the skin over evenly with your hands.

4 Place the chicken in a roasting pan and brush lightly with oil.

5 Roast the chicken in a preheated oven, 375°F/190°C, for 25 minutes per 1 lb/450 g plus 25 minutes, or until there is no trace of pink in the juices when the chicken is pierced through the thickest part with a skewer. If the breast starts to brown too much, cover the chicken with foil.

6 Melt the butter in a skillet and sauté the sliced apple in the butter until golden. Stir in the redcurrant jelly and warm through until melted. Garnish the chicken with the apple slices and serve with mixed vegetables.

NUTRITION

Calories *219*; Sugars *7 g*; Protein *29 g*; Carbohydrate *9 g*; Fat *8 g*; Saturates *4 g*

easy

10 mins

2 hrs 15 mins

The richness of the duck meat contrasts well with the apricot sauce. If duckling portions are unavailable, use a whole bird cut into portions.

Roast Duck *with* Apple

1 Place the duck on a wire rack over a roasting pan and prick all over with a fork or a large needle.

2 Brush the duck with the soy sauce. Sprinkle with the sugar and season with pepper. Roast in a preheated oven, 375°F/190°C, basting occasionally, for 50–60 minutes, until the meat is cooked through—the juices should run clear when a skewer is inserted into the thickest part of the meat.

3 Place the apples in a small roasting pan and mix with the lemon juice and honey. Add a few bay leaves and season with salt and pepper to taste. Cook alongside the duck, basting occasionally, for 20–25 minutes, until tender. Discard the bay leaves.

4 To make the sauce, place the apricots in a blender or food processor with the juice from the can and the sherry. Process for a few seconds until smooth. Alternatively, mash the apricots with a fork until smooth and mix with the juice and sherry.

5 Just before serving, heat the apricot paste in a small pan. Serve the duck with the apple wedges, apricot sauce, and fresh vegetables. (Remove the skin from the duck and pat the flesh with paper towels to absorb any excess fat, if liked.)

SERVES 4

4 duckling portions, about 12 oz/350 g each, trimmed
4 tbsp dark soy sauce
2 tbsp light brown sugar
2 red-skinned dessert apples
2 green-skinned dessert apples
juice of 1 lemon
2 tbsp clear honey
a few bay leaves
salt and pepper
mixed fresh vegetables, to serve

sauce

14 oz/400 g canned apricots, in natural juice
4 tbsp sweet sherry

NUTRITION

Calories *316*; Sugars *38 g*; Protein *25 g*; Carbohydrate *40 g*; Fat *6 g*; Saturates *1 g*

moderate

10 mins
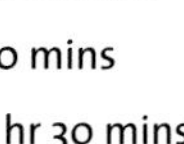
1 hr 30 mins

The tartness of citrus fruit goes well with the rich meat of duckling. Duckling makes a delightful change from chicken for the barbecue grill.

Citrus Duckling Skewers

SERVES 4

3 skinless, boneless duckling breasts, cut into bite-sized pieces
1 small red onion, cut into wedges
1 small eggplant, cut into cubes
lime or lemon wedges, to garnish (optional)

marinade

grated peel and juice of 1 lemon
grated peel and juice of 1 lime
grated peel and juice of 1 orange
1 garlic clove, crushed
1 tsp dried oregano
2 tbsp olive oil
dash of Tabasco sauce

1 Place the duckling in a nonmetallic bowl with the prepared vegetables.

2 To make the marinade, place all the ingredients for the marinade in a screw-top jar and shake until well combined. Pour the marinade over the duckling and vegetables and toss to coat. Set aside to marinate in the refrigerator for 30 minutes.

3 Remove the duckling and vegetables from the marinade and thread them in alternate pieces onto pre-soaked wooden skewers, reserving the marinade.

4 Grill the skewers on an oiled rack over medium-hot coals, turning and basting frequently with the reserved marinade, for 15-20 minutes, until the meat is cooked through. Alternatively, cook under a preheated broiler.

5 Serve the kabobs immediately, garnished with lime wedges for squeezing, if using.

NUTRITION

Calories *205*; Sugars *5 g*; Protein *24 g*; Carbohydrate *5 g*; Fat *10 g*; Saturates *2 g*

easy
45 mins
20 mins

COOK'S TIP

For more zing, add 1 teaspoon of chile sauce to the marinade. The meat can be marinated for several hours, but it is best to marinate the vegetables separately for about 30 minutes.

Prepare these steaks the day before they are needed and serve in toasted ciabatta bread, accompanied by crisp salad greens.

Glazed Turkey Steaks

1 Place the redcurrant jelly and lime juice in a pan and heat gently until the jelly melts. Add the oil, wine, ginger, and nutmeg.

2 Place the turkey steaks in a shallow, nonmetallic dish, and season with salt and pepper to taste. Pour the marinade over the turkey, turning the meat so that it is well coated. Cover and chill overnight.

3 Remove the turkey, reserving the marinade for basting, and grill on an oiled rack over hot coals for about 4 minutes on each side. Baste the turkey steaks frequently with the reserved marinade.

4 Meanwhile, toss the salad greens in the vinaigrette dressing. Cut the ciabatta loaf in half lengthwise and place, cut-side down, at the side of the barbecue grill. Cook until golden. Place each steak on top of a few salad greens, sandwiched between 2 pieces of bread, and serve immediately with cherry tomatoes.

SERVES 4

1/3 cup redcurrant jelly
2 tbsp lime juice
3 tbsp olive oil
2 tbsp dry white wine
1/4 tsp ground ginger
pinch of grated nutmeg
4 turkey breast steaks
salt and pepper

to serve

mixed salad greens
vinaigrette dressing
1 ciabatta loaf
cherry tomatoes

COOK'S TIP

Turkey and chicken scallops are also ideal for cooking on the barbecue grill. Leave them overnight in a marinade of your choice and cook, basting with a little lemon juice and oil.

NUTRITION

Calories *219*; Sugars *4 g*; Protein *28 g*; Carbohydrate *4 g*; Fat *10 g*; Saturates *1 g*

very easy

8 hrs 12 mins

15 mins

Fish *and* Seafood

Naturally low in fat, yet rich in minerals and proteins, white fish and shellfish are ideal to include in a low-fat diet. There are so many different textured and flavored fish available that they lend themselves to a wide range of cooking methods, as you will see from the recipes that follow. White fish such as cod, haddock, halibut, monkfish, and mullet are readily available and easy to cook. Shellfish such as shrimp, oysters, crab, and lobster may take a little longer to prepare, but are well worth the effort. Oily fish—like salmon, trout, tuna, and mackerel—are high in fat, albeit beneficial oils, and should be included in the diet, but eaten in moderation.

These shellfish and vegetable kabobs are ideal for parties. They are quick and easy to prepare and take little time to cook.

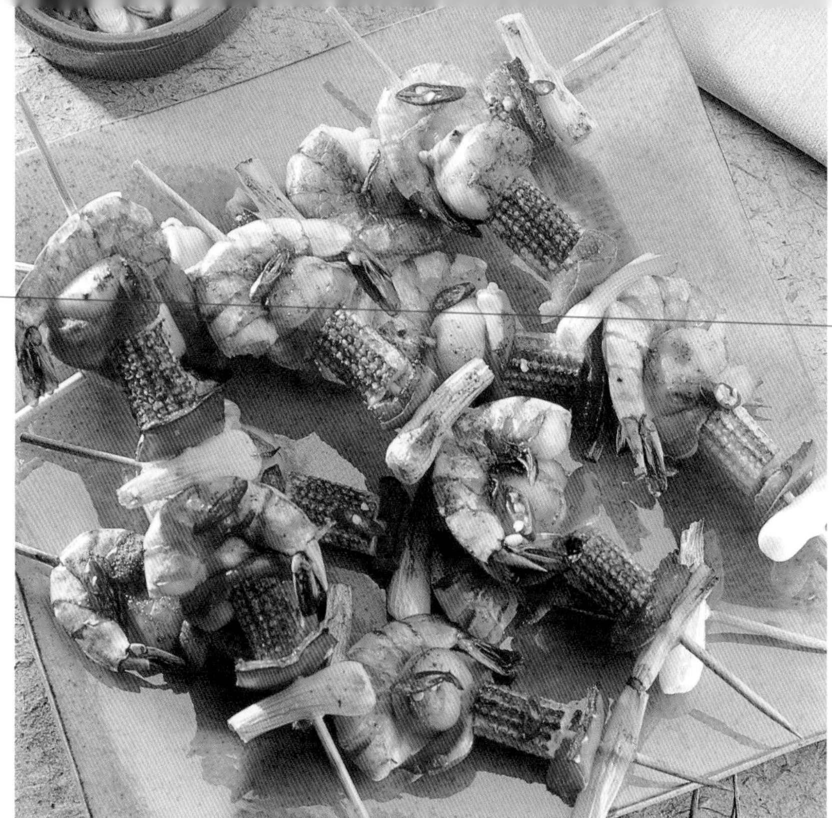

Asian Shellfish Kabobs

SERVES 4

12 oz/350 g raw jumbo shrimp, peeled leaving tails intact
12 oz/350 g scallops, trimmed and halved (cut into fourths if large)
1 bunch scallions, sliced into 1-inch/2.5-cm pieces
1 red bell pepper, halved, seeded, and cubed
3½ oz/100 g baby corn cobs, sliced into 1-cm/½-inch pieces
3 tbsp dark soy sauce
½ tsp hot chili powder
½ tsp ground ginger
1 tbsp sunflower oil
1 fresh red chile, seeded and sliced, to garnish

dip

4 tbsp dark soy sauce
4 tbsp dry sherry
2 tsp clear honey
1-inch/2.5-cm piece of fresh gingerroot, grated
1 scallion, sliced very finely

NUTRITION

Calories *93*; Sugars *1 g*; Protein *15 g*; Carbohydrate *2 g*; Fat *2 g*; Saturates *0.3 g*

moderate

2 hrs 30 mins

5 mins

1 Divide the shrimp, scallops, scallions, red bell pepper, and baby corn into 12 portions and thread onto pre-soaked wooden skewers. Cover the ends of the skewers with foil so that they do not burn and place in a shallow dish.

2 Mix together the soy sauce, chili powder, and ginger and brush the mixture over the kabobs. Cover and chill for about 2 hours.

3 Preheat the broiler to hot. Arrange the kabobs on the rack, brush with oil and cook for 2–3 minutes on each side until the shrimp turn pink, the scallops become opaque, and the vegetables have softened.

4 Mix together the ingredients for the dip in a bowl.

5 Remove the foil and transfer the kabobs to a warm serving platter. Garnish with sliced chile and serve with the dip.

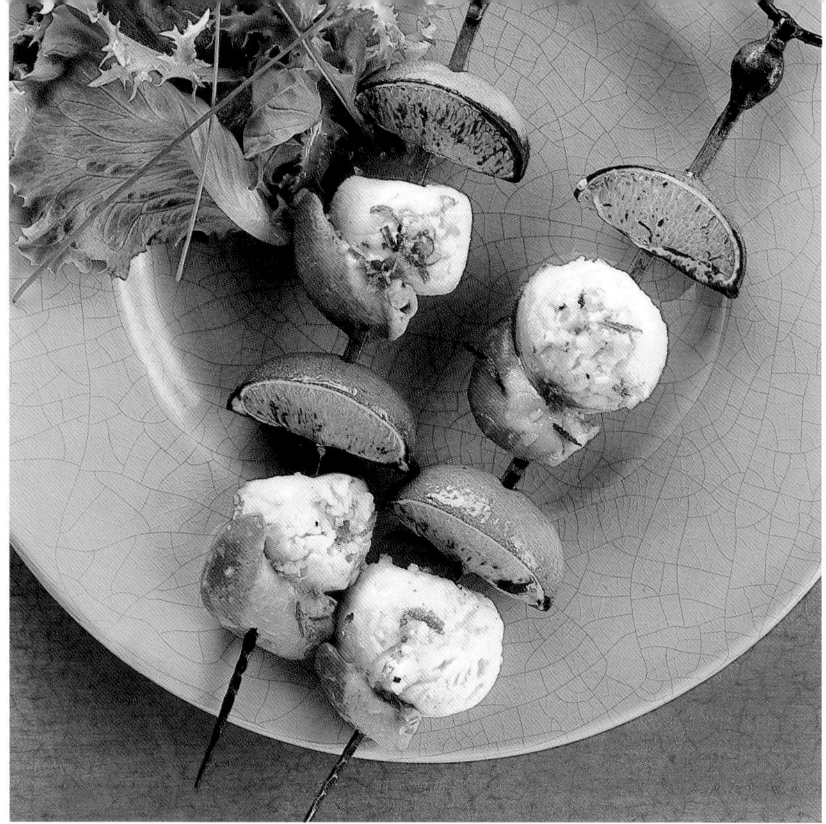

Since the scallops are marinated, it is not essential that they are fresh; frozen shellfish are fine for a barbecue grill.

Scallop Skewers

1 If using wooden skewers, soak 8 skewers in warm water for at least 10 minutes to prevent the food from sticking and the skewers from burning.

2 Combine the lime peel and juice, lemongrass, garlic, and chile together in a pestle and mortar or spice grinder to make a paste.

3 Thread 2 scallops with the corals onto each of the 8 skewers, alternating with the lime wedges. Cover the ends of the skewers with foil to prevent them from burning.

4 To make the dressing, whisk together the oil and lemon juice, and season with salt and pepper to taste.

5 Coat the scallops with the spice paste and cook for 10 minutes over a medium-hot barbecue grill, basting occasionally. Turn the skewers once.

6 Toss the arugula, mixed salad greens, and dressing together in a bowl.

7 Serve the scallops piping hot, 2 skewers on each plate, with the salad.

COOK'S TIP

Ask your fishstore to prepare the scallops for you, if using fresh ones.

SERVES 4

grated peel and juice of 2 limes
2 tbsp chopped finely lemongrass or 1 tbsp lemon juice
2 garlic cloves, crushed
1 fresh green chile, seeded and chopped
16 scallops, with corals
2 limes, each cut into 8 segments

dressing

2 tbsp sunflower oil
1 tbsp lemon juice
salt and pepper

to serve

1 cup arugula salad
3 cups mixed salad greens

NUTRITION

Calories *182*; Sugars *0 g*; Protein *29 g*; Carbohydrate *0 g*; Fat *7 g*; Saturates *1 g*

easy

30 mins

10 mins

The Japanese sauce used here goes particularly well with salmon, although it is usually served with chicken.

Salmon Yakitori

SERVES 4

12 oz/350 g chunky salmon fillet, cut into 2-inch/5-cm chunks
8 baby leeks, cut into 2-inch/5-cm lengths

yakitori sauce

5 tbsp light soy sauce
5 tbsp Fresh Fish Bouillon (see page 14)
2 tbsp superfine sugar
5 tbsp dry white wine
3 tbsp sweet sherry
1 garlic clove, crushed

1 Thread the salmon and leeks alternately on to 8 pre-soaked wooden skewers. Leave to chill in the refrigerator until required.

2 To make the sauce, place all of the ingredients in a small pan and heat gently, stirring, until the sugar has dissolved.

3 Bring to a boil, then reduce the heat and simmer for 2 minutes. Strain the sauce through a fine strainer and leave to cool until it is required.

4 Pour about one-third of the sauce into a small dish and set aside to serve with the kabobs.

5 Brush plenty of the remaining sauce over the skewers and cook directly on the barbecue grill rack. (If preferred, place a sheet of oiled foil on the rack and cook the salmon on that.)

6 Grill the salmon and leek kabobs over hot coals for about 10 minutes, or until cooked through, turning once.

7 Baste the kabobs frequently during cooking with the sauce to prevent them drying out. Transfer the kabobs to a large serving platter and serve with a small bowl of the reserved sauce for dipping.

NUTRITION

Calories *247*; Sugars *10 g*; Protein *19 g*; Carbohydrate *12 g*; Fat *11 g*; Saturates *2 g*

 easy

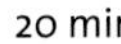

 20 mins

15 mins

A simple basting sauce is brushed over these tasty kabobs. When served with crusty bread and salad greens, they make a perfect light meal.

Lemon Monkfish Skewers

1 Thread the monkfish, zucchini, lemon, tomatoes, and bay leaves onto 4 pre-soaked wooden or metal skewers, alternating each ingredient to make the skewers look colorful.

2 To make the basting sauce, combine the oil, lemon juice, thyme, lemon pepper, and season with salt to taste in a small bowl.

3 Baste the skewers liberally and cook them on the barbecue grill over medium–hot coals for about 15 minutes, basting frequently with the sauce until the fish is cooked through.

4 Transfer the skewers to plates and serve with salad greens and chunks of fresh crusty bread.

SERVES 4

1 lb/450 g monkfish tail, cut into 2-inch/5-cm chunks
2 zucchini, sliced thickly
1 lemon, cut into wedges
12 cherry tomatoes
8 bay leaves

sauce

3 tbsp olive oil
2 tbsp lemon juice
1 tsp chopped fresh thyme
½ tsp lemon pepper
salt

to serve

salad greens
fresh crusty bread

NUTRITION

Calories *191*; Sugars *2 g*; Protein *21 g*; Carbohydrate *1 g*; Fat *11 g*; Saturates *1 g*

easy

10 mins

15 mins

COOK'S TIP

Use flounder fillets instead of the monkfish, if preferred. Allow 2 fillets per person, and skin and cut each fillet lengthwise into two. Roll up each piece and thread them onto the skewers.

This is a wonderful recipe for a special occasion dish. Cooked with cilantro and tomatoes, the scallops have a spicy flavor.

Balti Scallops

SERVES 4

1 lb 10 oz/750 g fresh scallops
2 tbsp oil
2 onions, chopped
3 tomatoes, quartered
2 fresh green chiles, sliced
lime wedges, to garnish

marinade

3 tbsp chopped fresh cilantro
1-inch/2.5-cm piece of fresh gingerroot, grated
1 tsp ground coriander
3 tbsp lemon juice
grated rind of 1 lemon
¼ tsp pepper
½ tsp salt
½ tsp ground cumin
1 garlic clove, crushed

1. To make the marinade, mix together the ingredients in a bowl.
2. Put the scallops into a bowl. Add the marinade and turn the scallops until they are well coated. Cover and leave to marinate for 1 hour, or overnight in the refrigerator.
3. Heat the oil in a Balti pan or wok, add the onions and cook until softened.
4. Add the tomatoes and chiles and cook for 1 minute.
5. Add the scallops and cook for 6–8 minutes, until the scallops are cooked through, but still succulent inside.
6. Serve garnished with lime wedges.

NUTRITION

Calories *258*; Sugars *2 g*; Protein *44 g*; Carbohydrate *3 g*; Fat *8 g*; Saturates *1 g*

easy

1 hr 15 mins–8 hrs

15 mins

COOK'S TIP

It is best to buy the scallops fresh in the shell with the roe. You will need about 3 lb 5 oz/1.5 kg and ask your fishmonger to clean them and remove the shell for you.

Herbs, onion, green bell pepper, and pumpkin seeds are used to flavor this baked fish dish, which is first marinated in fresh lime juice.

Yucatan Fish

1 Place the cod in a shallow, ovenproof dish and pour the lime juice over. Turn the fish in the juice, season with salt and pepper to taste, cover and refrigerate for 15–30 minutes.

2 Place the green bell pepper under a preheated moderate broiler. Broil, skin-side upwards, until it begins to char and blister. Leave to cool slightly, then peel off the skin and chop the flesh.

3 Heat the oil in a skillet and cook the onion, garlic, green pepper, and pumpkin seeds gently for 5 minutes, until the onion has softened.

4 Stir in the lime peel, cilantro, mixed herbs, mushrooms, and seasoning, and spoon the mixture over the fish.

5 Spoon the orange juice over the fish, cover with foil or a lid and place in a preheated oven, 350°F/180°C, for about 30 minutes, or until the fish is just tender.

6 Garnish the fish with lime wedges, if using, and fresh herbs, then serve.

SERVES 4

4 cod cutlets, steaks or hake cutlets, about 6 oz/175 g each
2 tbsp lime juice
1 green bell pepper, halved and seeded
1 tbsp olive oil
1 onion, chopped finely
1–2 garlic cloves, crushed
1½ oz/40 g green pumpkin seeds
grated peel of ½ lime
1 tbsp chopped fresh cilantro or parsley
1 tbsp chopped fresh mixed herbs
scant 1 cup thinly sliced white mushrooms
2–3 tbsp fresh orange juice or white wine
salt and pepper

to garnish
lime wedges (optional)
fresh mixed herbs

NUTRITION
Calories *248*; Sugars *2 g*; Protein *33 g*; Carbohydrate *3 g*; Fat *11 g*; Saturates *1 g*

moderate
30–40 mins
35 mins

This is a fiery recipe with subtle undertones. Since the flavor of the shrimp should still be noticeable, the spices should not dominate this dish.

Shrimp Bhuna

SERVES 4

2 dried red chilies, seeded if desired
3 fresh green chiles, chopped finely
1 tsp ground turmeric
½ tsp pepper
1 tsp paprika
3 garlic cloves, crushed
2 tsp white wine vinegar
½ tsp salt
1 lb 2 oz/500 g peeled, raw jumbo shrimp
3 tbsp vegetable oil
1 onion, chopped very finely
¾ cup water
2 tbsp lemon juice
2 tsp garam masala
fresh cilantro sprigs, to garnish

1 Combine the red chilies, green chiles, spices, garlic, vinegar, and salt in a nonmetallic bowl. Stir in the shrimp and set aside for 10 minutes.

2 Heat the oil in a preheated wok or large skillet. Add the onion, and cook, stirring occasionally, for 3–4 minutes, until soft.

3 Add the shrimp and the spice mixture to the wok and cook over a high heat for 2 minutes. Reduce the heat, add the water, and boil for 10 minutes, stirring occasionally, until the water has evaporated.

4 Stir in the lemon juice and garam masala, then transfer the mixture to a warm serving dish, and garnish with sprigs of cilantro.

NUTRITION

Calories *141* Sugars *0.4 g*; Protein *19 g*; Carbohydrate *1 g*; Fat *7 g*; Saturates *1 g*

very easy

15 mins

20 mins

COOK'S TIP

Garam masala should be used sparingly and is generally added to foods toward the end of their cooking time. It is also sprinkled over cooked meats, vegetables, and beans as a garnish.

Tuna has a firm flesh, which is ideal for barbecue grilling, but it can be a little dry unless it is marinated first.

Charred Tuna Steaks

SERVES 4

4 tuna steaks
3 tbsp light soy sauce
1 tbsp Worcestershire sauce
1 tsp wholegrain mustard
1 tsp superfine sugar
1 tbsp sunflower oil
salad greens, to serve

to garnish
fresh flatleaf parsley sprigs
lemon wedges

1 Place the tuna steaks in a single layer in a shallow dish.

2 Combine the light soy sauce, Worcestershire sauce, mustard, sugar, and oil in a small bowl. Pour the marinade over the tuna steaks. Gently turn the tuna steaks to coat well.

3 Cover with plastic wrap and set aside in the refrigerator to marinate for at least 30 minutes, or up to 2 hours.

4 Remove the tuna steaks from the marinade, reserving it for basting. Grill over hot coals for about 10–15 minutes, turning once and basting frequently with the reserved marinade.

5 Transfer the tuna steaks to warm serving plates. Garnish with flatleaf parsley and lemon wedges and serve immediately with salad greens.

NUTRITION

Calories *153* Sugars *1 g*; Protein *29 g*; Carbohydrate *1 g*; Fat *3 g*; Saturates *1 g*

 very easy

 2 hrs 10 mins

15 mins

COOK'S TIP

If a marinade contains soy sauce, the marinating time should be limited, usually to 2 hours to prevent the fish from drying out and becoming tough.

Salmon steaks, poached in a well-flavored bouillon and served with a piquant sauce, make a delicious light summer lunch or supper dish.

Poached Salmon

SERVES 4

1 small onion, sliced
1 small carrot, sliced
1 celery stalk, sliced
1 bay leaf
peel and juice of ½ orange
a few fresh parsley stalks
salt
5–6 black peppercorns
3 cups water
4 salmon steaks, about 12 oz/350 g each
salad greens, to serve
lemon twists, to garnish

sauce

1 large avocado, peeled, pitted and chopped roughly
½ cup low-fat plain yogurt
grated peel and juice of ½ orange
black pepper
a few drops of hot red pepper sauce

1 Put the onion, carrot, celery, bay leaf, orange peel and juice, parsley stalks, salt, and peppercorns in a pan just large enough to take the salmon steaks in a single layer. Pour the water over, cover the pan and bring to a boil. Reduce the heat and simmer the bouillon for 20 minutes.

2 Arrange the salmon steaks in the pan, return the bouillon to a boil. Reduce the heat and simmer for 3 minutes. Cover the pan, remove from the heat and leave the salmon to cool in the bouillon.

3 To make the sauce, place the avocado in a blender or food processor with the yogurt, orange peel and juice. Process until smooth, then season with salt, pepper and hot pepper sauce to taste.

4 Using a draining spoon, remove the salmon steaks from the bouillon (reserve it to make fish soup or a sauce), skin them, and pat dry with paper towels.

5 Arrange the salmon steaks on serving plates and spoon a little of the sauce on top of each one and garnish with lemon twists. Serve with the salad greens and the remaining sauce.

NUTRITION

Calories *712*; Sugars *5 g*; Protein *66 g*; Carbohydrate *6 g*; Fat *47 g*; Saturates *9 g*

 very easy
10 mins
30 mins

The secret of this dish lies in the simple, fresh flavors which complement the richness of the grilled fish perfectly.

Mackerel *with* Lime

1 Sprinkle the mackerel with the ground spices and season with salt and pepper to taste. Sprinkle 1 teaspoon of the chopped cilantro inside the cavity of each fish.

2 Combine the remaining cilantro, chile, lime peel and juice, and the oil in a small bowl. Brush the mixture liberally over the fish.

3 Place the fish in a hinged rack. Barbecue grill over hot coals for 3–4 minutes on each side, turning the fish once. Brush frequently with the remaining basting mixture.

4 Transfer to individual plates and garnish with chile flowers, if using, and lime slices, and serve with salad greens.

SERVES 4

4 small mackerel, gutted and heads removed
1/4 tsp ground coriander
1/4 tsp ground cumin
4 sprigs of fresh cilantro
3 tbsp chopped fresh cilantro
1 fresh red chile, seeded and chopped
grated peel and juice of 1 lime
2 tbsp sunflower oil
salt and pepper
salad greens, to serve

to garnish
1 lime, sliced
chile flowers (optional)

NUTRITION
Calories *302*; Sugars *0 g*; Protein *21 g*; Carbohydrate *0 g*; Fat *24 g*; Saturates *4 g*

easy
 10 mins
 10 mins

COOK'S TIP

To make the chile flowers, cut the tip of 8 small chiles lengthwise into thin strips, leaving the chiles intact at the stem end. Remove the seeds and place the chiles in ice water until curled.

The firm, sweet flesh of the trout is enhanced by the spicy flavor of the marinade.

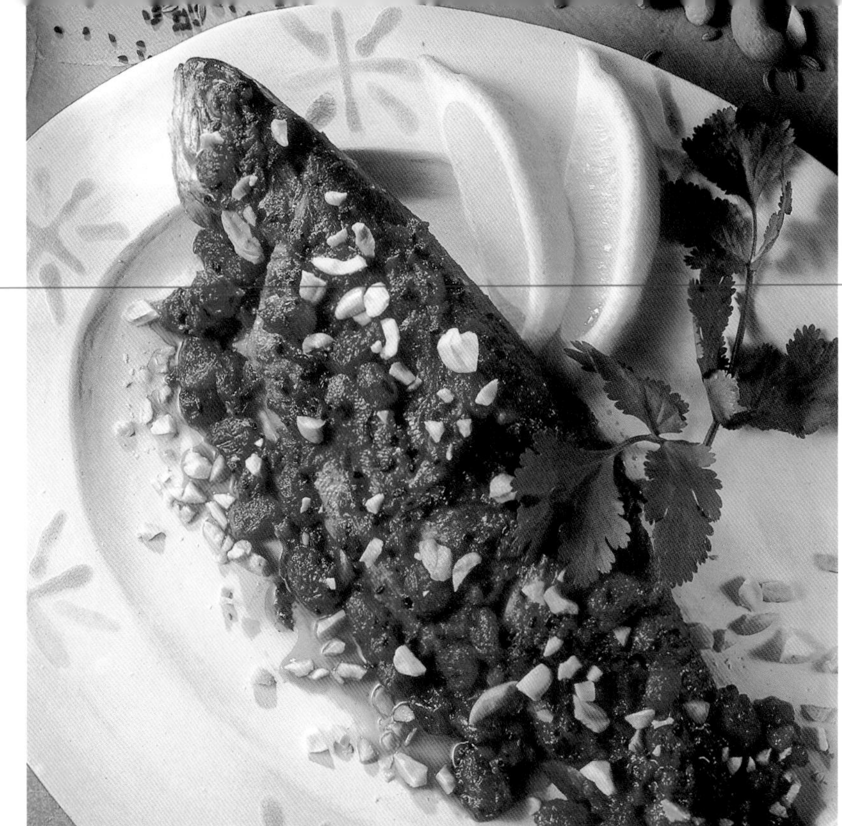

Delicately Spiced Trout

SERVES 4

4 trout, about 6–9 oz/175–250 g each, cleaned
3 tbsp oil
1 tsp fennel seeds
1 tsp onion seeds
1 garlic clove, crushed
2/3 cup coconut milk or fish bouillon
3 tbsp tomato paste
1/3 cup golden raisins
1/2 tsp garam masala

to garnish

1/4 cup chopped cashews
lemon wedges
fresh cilantro sprigs

marinade

4 tbsp lemon juice
2 tbsp chopped fresh cilantro
1 tsp ground cumin
1/2 tsp salt
1/2 tsp pepper

NUTRITION

Calories *374*; Sugars *13 g*; Protein *38 g*; Carbohydrate *14 g*; Fat *19 g*; Saturates *3 g*

easy
50 mins
20 mins

1 Slash the trout skin in several places on both sides with a sharp knife.

2 To make the marinade, mix all the ingredients together in a bowl.

3 Put the trout in a shallow dish and pour the marinade over. Leave to marinate for 30–40 minutes, turning the fish occasionally.

4 Heat the oil in a preheated wok or Balti pan and fry the fennel seeds and onion seeds until they start popping.

5 Add the garlic, coconut milk, and tomato paste and bring the mixture in the wok to a boil.

6 Add the golden raisins, garam masala, and trout to the wok with the juices from the marinade. Cover and simmer for 5 minutes. Turn the trout over and simmer for another 10 minutes.

7 Serve garnished with the cashews, lemon, and cilantro sprigs.

Sea bass is often paired with subtle Asian flavors. For a special occasion, you may like to bone the fish.

Baked Sea Bass

1 For each fish, lay out a double thickness of foil and oil the top piece well, or lay a piece of baking parchment over the foil.

2 Place the fish in the center of the foil and expose the cavities. Divide the scallion, ginger, and garlic between each cavity.

3 Pour the mirin over the fish and season with salt and pepper to taste .

4 Close the cavities and lay each fish on its side. Fold over the foil to encase the fish and seal the edges securely. Fold each end neatly.

5 Cook over a medium-hot barbecue grill for 15 minutes, turning once.

6 To serve, remove the foil and cut each fish into 2–3 pieces. Serve with the pickled ginger, if using, accompanied by soy sauce.

SERVES 4

2 sea bass, about 2 lb 4 oz/1 kg each, gutted and scaled
2 scallions, green part only, cut into strips
2-inch/5-cm piece of fresh gingerroot, cut into strips
2 garlic cloves, unpeeled, crushed lightly
2 tbsp mirin or dry sherry
salt and pepper

to serve

pickled sushi ginger (optional)
soy sauce

COOK'S TIP

Fresh sea bass is just as delicious when cooked very simply. Stuff the fish with garlic and chopped herbs, brush with olive oil, and bake in the oven.

NUTRITION

Calories *140*; Sugars *0.1 g*; Protein *29 g*; Carbohydrate *0.1 g*; Fat *1 g*; Saturates *0.2 g*

 easy

 10 mins

15 mins

A delicious aromatic coating of coconut and spices makes this dish rather special. Serve it with crisp salad greens and crusty bread.

Indonesian-Style Spicy Cod

SERVES 4

1 lemongrass stem, outer layer removed and thinly sliced
1 small red onion, chopped
3 garlic cloves, chopped
2 fresh red chiles, seeded and chopped
1 tsp grated fresh gingerroot
¼ tsp turmeric
2 tbsp butter, cut into small cubes
8 tbsp coconut milk
2 tbsp lemon juice
4 medium cod steaks
salt and pepper
salad greens, to serve
fresh red chiles, to garnish (optional)

1 Place the lemongrass, onion, garlic, chiles, ginger, and turmeric in a food processor and blend until the ingredients are finely chopped. Season with salt and pepper to taste.

2 With the processor running, add the butter, coconut milk, and lemon juice, and process until well blended.

3 Place the fish in a shallow, nonmetallic dish. Pour the coconut mixture over, and turn the fish to coat it evenly on both sides.

4 Place the fish steaks in a hinged rack, if you have one, or on a grill rack and cook over hot coals for 15 minutes, or until the fish is cooked through, turning once. Serve with salad greens, garnished with red chiles, if using.

NUTRITION

Calories *146*; Sugars *2 g*; Protein *19 g*; Carbohydrate *2 g*; Fat *7 g*; Saturates *4 g*

 easy
10 mins
15 mins

COOK'S TIP

If you prefer a milder flavor, omit the chiles altogether. For a hotter flavor do not remove the seeds from one or both of the chiles.

The marinade for this dish has a distinctly Japanese flavor. Its subtle taste goes particularly well with any type of white fish.

Japanese Flounder

1 Make a few slashes down the sides of each fish so that they absorb the flavors of the marinade.

2 Mix together the soy sauce, sake, sesame oil, lemon juice, sugar, ginger, and garlic in a large, shallow dish.

3 Place the fish in the marinade and turn to coat them on both sides. Leave to marinate in the refrigerator for 1 hour.

4 Grill the fish over hot coals for about 10 minutes, turning once.

5 Transfer the fish to a serving dish and garnish with the carrot and scallions. Serve immediately.

SERVES 4

4 small flounders
6 tbsp soy sauce
2 tbsp sake or dry white wine
2 tbsp sesame oil
1 tbsp lemon juice
2 tbsp light muscovado sugar
1 tsp grated fresh gingerroot
1 garlic clove, crushed

to garnish

1 small carrot, cut into thin strips
4 scallions, cut into thin strips

COOK'S TIP

Use sole instead of the flounders and scatter over some toasted sesame seeds instead of the carrot and scallions, if preferred.

NUTRITION

Calories *207*; Sugars *9 g*; Protein *22 g*; Carbohydrate *10 g*; Fat *8 g*; Saturates *1 g*

 easy

1 hr 15 mins

10 mins

Here, herrings are filled with an orange-flavored stuffing and are wrapped in foil before being baked on the barbecue grill.

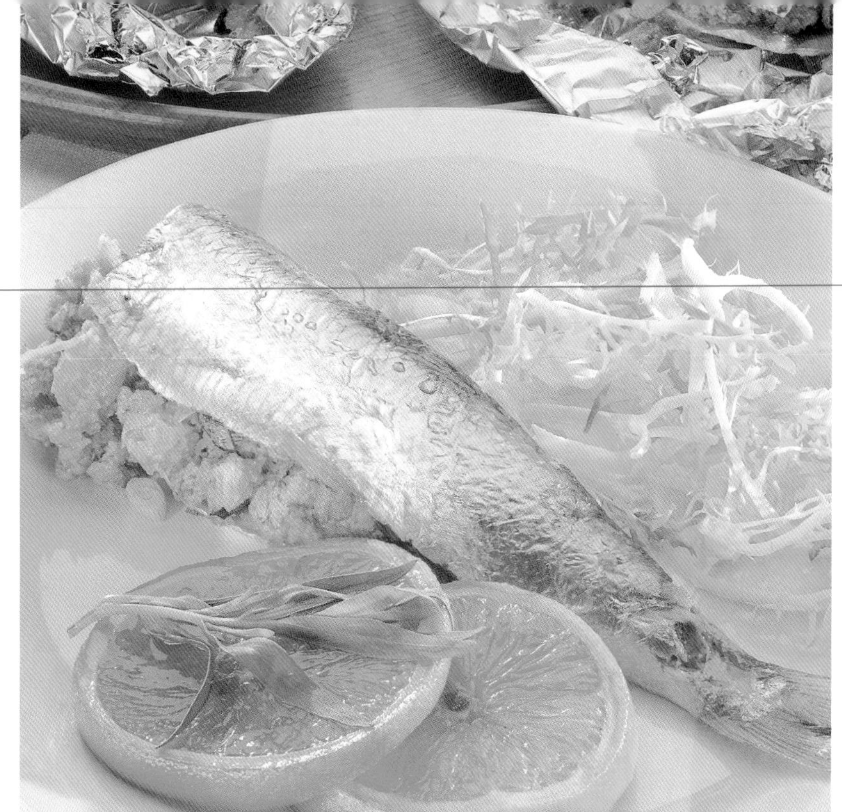

Herrings *with* Tarragon

SERVES 4

4 herrings, gutted and headed
salt and pepper
salad greens, to serve

stuffing

1 orange
4 scallions, chopped finely
4 tbsp fresh whole-wheat bread crumbs
1 tbsp chopped fresh tarragon

to garnish

1 tbsp light brown sugar
2 oranges, sliced thickly
1 tbsp olive oil
fresh tarragon sprigs

1 To make the stuffing, pare the peel from half of the orange, using a zester. Peel and chop the orange flesh on a plate, to catch the juices.

2 Mix together the orange flesh, juice, peel, scallions, bread crumbs, and tarragon in a bowl. Season with salt and pepper to taste.

3 Divide the stuffing into 4 equal portions and use it to fill the body cavities of the fish.

4 Place each fish on to a square of lightly greased foil and wrap the foil around them to enclose them completely. Grill over hot coals for 20–30 minutes, until cooked through—the flesh should be white and firm to the touch.

5 Meanwhile make the garnish. Sprinkle the sugar over the slices of orange.

6 Just before the fish is cooked, drizzle a little oil over the orange slices and chargrill for 5 minutes to heat through.

7 Transfer the stuffed herrings to serving plates and garnish with the cooked orange slices and fresh tarragon sprigs. Serve with fresh salad greens.

NUTRITION

Calories *332*; Sugars *4 g*; Protein *21 g*; Carbohydrate *9 g*; Fat *24 g*; Saturates *6 g*

easy
15 mins
35 mins

Red mullet may be used instead of the snapper, although their size makes them a little more difficult to stuff. Use one mullet per person.

Steamed Stuffed Snapper

1 Blanch the spinach for 40 seconds, rinse in cold water, and drain well, pressing out as much moisture as possible.

2 Arrange the spinach on a heatproof plate and place the fish on top.

3 To make the stuffing, combine the cooked rice, ginger, scallions, soy sauce, sesame oil, star anise, and orange in a bowl.

4 Spoon the rice stuffing into the body cavity of the fish, pressing it in well with a spoon.

5 Cover the plate and cook in a steamer for 10 minutes, or until the fish is cooked through.

6 Garnish the fish with orange slices and scallions and serve.

SERVES 4

6 oz/175 g spinach leaves
3 lb/1.3 kg whole snapper, gutted and scaled

stuffing

1/3 cup cooked long-grain rice
1 tsp grated fresh gingerroot
2 scallions, chopped finely
2 tsp light soy sauce
1 tsp sesame oil
1/2 tsp ground star anise
1 orange, segmented and chopped

to garnish

orange slices
shredded scallions

NUTRITION

Calories *406*; Sugars *4 g*; Protein *68 g*; Carbohydrate *9 g*; Fat *9 g*; Saturates *0 g*

easy

20 mins

10 mins

COOK'S TIP

The name "snapper" covers a family of tropical and subtropical fish that vary in color. They may be red, orange, pink, gray, or blue-green and almost all have a fine flavor. They range in size from 6 inches/15 cm to 3 ft/90 cm.

Liven up firm steaks of white fish with a spicy, colorful relish. Use red onions for a slightly sweeter flavor.

Pan-Seared Halibut

SERVES 4

1 tsp olive oil
4 halibut steaks, about 6 oz/175 g each, skinned
½ tsp cornstarch
2 tsp cold water
salt and pepper
2 tbsp snipped fresh chives, to garnish

red onion relish

2 red onions, sliced thinly
6 shallots, sliced thinly
1 tbsp lemon juice
2 tsp olive oil
2 tbsp red wine vinegar
2 tsp superfine sugar
⅔ cup Fresh Fish Bouillon (see page 14)

1 To make the relish, place the onions and shallots in a small bowl and toss in the lemon juice.

2 Heat the oil in a heavy-based skillet and cook the onions and shallots for 3–4 minutes, until just softened.

3 Add the vinegar and sugar and cook for another 2 minutes over a high heat. Pour in the bouillon and season with salt and pepper to taste. Bring to a boil, then reduce the heat, and simmer gently for another 8–9 minutes, until the sauce has thickened and slightly reduced.

4 Brush a non-slip, ridged skillet with oil and heat until hot. Press the fish steaks into the pan to sear, reduce the heat and cook for 4 minutes. Turn the fish over and cook for 4–5 minutes, until cooked through. Drain on paper towels and keep warm.

5 Mix the cornstarch with the water to make a smooth paste and stir it into the onion relish and heat through, stirring, until thickened. Season to taste.

6 Pile the relish onto 4 warm serving plates and place a halibut steak on top of each. Garnish with fresh chives.

NUTRITION

Calories *197*; Sugars *1 g*; Protein *31 g*; Carbohydrate *2 g*; Fat *7 g*; Saturates *1 g*

 moderate

 30 mins

30 mins

COOK'S TIP

If raw onions make your eyes water, try peeling them under cold, running water. Alternatively, stand back from the onion so that your face isn't directly over it when peeling.

A delicate dish comprising sole fillets rolled up with spinach and shrimp, and served in a rich and creamy ginger sauce.

Sole Paupiettes

1 Season the fish fillets and divide the spinach between them, laying the leaves on the skin side. Divide half of the shrimp between them. Roll up the fillets from head to tail, enclosing the spinach and shrimp, and secure with wooden cocktail sticks. Arrange the rolls on a plate in the base of a bamboo steamer.

2 Stand a low metal trivet in a wok and add enough water to come almost to the top of it, then bring to a boil. Place the bamboo steamer on the trivet, cover with the steamer lid and then the wok lid, or cover tightly with a domed piece of foil. Steam gently for 30 minutes, until the fish is tender and cooked through.

3 Remove the fish rolls and keep warm. Empty the wok and wipe dry with paper towels. Heat the oil in the wok, swirling it around until really hot. Add the scallions and ginger and stir-fry for 1–2 minutes.

4 Add the bouillon to the wok and bring to a boil. Blend the cornstarch with the cream. Add the yogurt and remaining shrimp to the wok and heat gently, until boiling. Add a little sauce to the blended cream and return it to the wok. Heat gently until thickened and season with salt and pepper.

5 Serve the paupiettes with the sauce spooned over, garnished with whole shrimp, if using.

SERVES 4

- 2 Dover sole, large lemon sole, or flounder, filleted
- 4½ oz/125 g baby spinach leaves
- 4½ oz /125 g peeled, cooked shrimp, thawed if frozen
- 2 tsp sunflower oil
- 2–4 scallions, sliced finely, diagonally
- 2 thin slices of fresh gingerroot, chopped finely
- ⅔ cup Fresh Fish Bouillon (see page 14) or water
- 2 tsp cornstarch
- 4 tbsp light cream
- 6 tbsp low-fat plain yogurt
- salt and pepper
- whole cooked shrimp, to garnish (optional)

NUTRITION

Calories *253*; Sugars *7 g*; Protein *24 g*; Carbohydrate *9 g*; Fat *14 g*; Saturates *5 g*

 challenging

10 mins

45 mins

This flavorsome, colorful fish pie is perfect for a light supper. The addition of smoked salmon gives it a touch of luxury.

Smoky Fish Pie

SERVES 4

2 lb/900 g smoked haddock or cod fillets
2½ cups skim milk
2 bay leaves
1½ cups quartered white mushrooms
1 cup frozen peas
⅔ cup frozen corn kernels
4 cups diced potatoes
5 tbsp low-fat plain yogurt
4 tbsp chopped fresh parsley
2 oz/55 g smoked salmon, sliced thin strips
3 tbsp cornstarch
¼ cup grated smoked cheese
salt and pepper

NUTRITION

Calories *523*; Sugars *15 g*; Protein *58 g*; Carbohydrate *63 g*; Fat *6 g*; Saturates *2 g*

 challenging

20 mins

50–55 mins

1 Place the fish in a large pan and add the milk and bay leaves, then bring to a boil. Reduce the heat, cover, and simmer gently for 5 minutes.

2 Add the mushrooms, peas, and corn, return to a simmer, cover, and cook for 5–7 minutes. Let cool.

3 Place the potatoes in a pan, cover with water, bring to a boil, and cook for 8 minutes, until tender. Drain well and mash with a fork or a potato masher. Stir in the yogurt and parsley, and season with salt and pepper to taste. Set aside.

4 Using a draining spoon, remove the fish from the pan. Flake the cooked fish, removing the skin and any bones, and place the fish in an ovenproof gratin dish. Reserve the cooking liquid.

5 Drain the vegetables, reserving the cooking liquid, and gently stir into the fish with the salmon strips.

6 Blend a little cooking liquid into the cornstarch to make a paste. Transfer the rest of the liquid to a pan and add the paste. Heat through, stirring, until thickened. Discard the bay leaves and season to taste. Pour the sauce over the fish and vegetables and mix.

7 Spoon the mashed potato over the fish so that it is covered, sprinkle with cheese, and bake in a preheated oven, 400°F/200°C, for 25–30 minutes, until golden.

This makes a change from the standard pizza toppings—the base is piled high with seafood and baked with a red bell pepper and tomato sauce.

Seafood Pizza

1 Place the pizza dough mix in a bowl and stir in the dill. Make the dough according to the package instructions.

2 Press the dough into a circle measuring about 10 inches/25 cm across on a cookie sheet lined with baking parchment. Cover with a dish cloth and set aside to rise.

3 To make the sauce, arrange the red bell pepper on a broiler rack. Cook under a preheated broiler for 8–10 minutes, until softened and charred. Let cool slightly, peel off the skin, and chop the flesh.

4 Place the tomatoes and bell pepper in a heavy-based pan. Bring to a boil and simmer over a low heat for 10 minutes. Stir in the tomato paste and season with salt and pepper to taste.

5 Spread the sauce evenly over the pizza dough and top with the seafood. Sprinkle with the capers and olives, top with the grated cheeses and bake in a preheated oven, 400°F/200°C, for 25–30 minutes. Garnish with sprigs of fresh dill sprigs and serve hot.

COOK'S TIP

As an alternative to the pizza dough mix, use ready-made pizza bases and brush with a little dill-infused oil.

SERVES 4

5 oz/140 g standard pizza dough mix
4 tbsp chopped fresh dill or 2 tbsp dried dill
fresh dill sprigs, to garnish

sauce

1 large red bell pepper, halved and seeded
14 oz/400 g canned chopped tomatoes with onion and herbs
3 tbsp tomato paste
salt and pepper

topping

12 oz/350 g assorted cooked seafood, thawed if frozen
1 tbsp capers in brine, drained
1 oz/25 g pitted black olives in brine, drained
¼ cup grated low-fat mozzarella cheese
¼ cup freshly grated Parmesan cheese

NUTRITION

Calories *248*; Sugars *7 g*; Protein *27 g*; Carbohydrate *22 g*; Fat *6 g*; Saturates *1 g*

 challenging
40 mins
45–50 mins

Vegetables *and* Salads

There is more to the vegetarian diet than lentil roast and nut cutlets. For those of you who have cut out meat and fish completely from your diet, or if you just want to reduce your intake of these ingredients, this chapter offers an exciting assortment of low-fat vegetarian dishes, ranging from pizzas, to curries, and bakes. The advantage of vegetable dishes is that very often they are lower in fat, and the ingredients can be varied according to personal preference or seasonal availability. Always remember to buy the freshest vegetables available to ensure maximum flavor.

These grilled tomato cups are filled with a delicious Greek-style combination of herbs, nuts, and raisins.

Stuffed Tomatoes

SERVES 4

4 beefsteak tomatoes, halved and seeded
5 cups cooked rice
8 scallions, chopped
3 tbsp chopped fresh mint
2 tbsp chopped fresh parsley
3 tbsp pine nuts
3 tbsp raisins
2 tsp olive oil
salt and pepper

1 Stand the tomatoes upside down on paper towels for a few minutes to let the juices drain out. Turn the tomato shells the right way up and sprinkle the insides with salt and pepper.

2 Mix together the rice, scallions, mint, parsley, pine nuts, and raisins, then divide the rice mixture between the tomato cups.

3 Drizzle a little olive oil over the stuffed tomatoes, then cook on an oiled rack over medium-hot coals for about 10 minutes, until they are tender and cooked through.

4 Transfer the tomatoes to serving plates and serve immediately.

NUTRITION

Calories *156*; Sugars *10 g*; Protein *3 g*; Carbohydrate *22 g*; Fat *7 g*; Saturates *0.7 g*

 easy
 10 mins
 10 mins

COOK'S TIP

Tomatoes are a popular barbecue grill vegetable. Try broiling slices of beefsteak tomato and onion, brushed with a little oil, and topped with fresh herb sprigs, or thread cherry tomatoes onto skewers and grill for 5–10 minutes.

Soft, creamy rice combines with the flavors of citrus and light anise to make this a delicious supper or a substantial appetizer for six hungry people.

Fragrant Asparagus Risotto

1 Bring a small pan of water to a boil and cook the asparagus for 1 minute. Drain and set aside.

2 Pour the bouillon into a pan and bring to a boil, then reduce the heat and maintain a gentle simmer.

3 Carefully melt the low-fat spread with the oil in a large pan, taking care that the water in the low-fat spread does not evaporate, and gently cook the fennel, celery, and leeks for 3–4 minutes, until just softened. Add the rice and cook, stirring, for another 2 minutes, until combined.

4 Add a ladleful of bouillon to the pan and cook gently, stirring, until absorbed.

5 Continue adding the bouillon to the rice, a ladleful at a time, until the rice becomes creamy, thick, and tender. This process will take about 25 minutes and should not be hurried.

6 Finely grate the peel and extract the juice from 1 orange and mix into the rice. Carefully remove the peel and pith from the remaining oranges. Holding the fruit over the pan, cut out the orange segments and add to the rice, along with any juice that falls.

7 Stir the orange into the rice, along with the asparagus. Season with salt and pepper to taste and garnish with the fennel fronds.

SERVES 4

4 oz/115 g fine asparagus spears, trimmed
5 cups Fresh Vegetable Bouillon (see page 14)
2 tbsp low-fat spread
1 tsp olive oil
2 fennel bulbs, thinly sliced, fronds reserved
2 celery stalks, chopped
2 leeks, shredded
3 cups risotto rice
3 oranges
salt and pepper

NUTRITION

Calories *223*; Sugars *9 g*; Protein *6 g*; Carbohydrate *40 g*; Fat *6 g*; Saturates *1 g*

 moderate
10 mins
35 mins

Ready-made individual pizza doughs are covered with a chile-tomato sauce and topped with kidney beans, cheese, and jalapeño chiles.

Mexican-Style Pizzas

SERVES 4

4 ready-made, precooked individual pizza crusts
1 tbsp olive oil
1 cup canned chopped tomatoes with garlic and herbs
2 tbsp tomato paste
1 cup canned kidney beans, drained and rinsed
⅔ cup corn kernels, thawed if frozen
1–2 tsp chile sauce
1 large red onion, shredded
1 cup grated reduced-fat, sharp Colby cheese
1 large green chile, seeded and sliced into rings
salt and pepper

1 Arrange the pizza crusts on a cookie sheet and brush the tops lightly with the olive oil.

2 Combine the tomatoes, tomato paste, kidney beans, and corn kernels in a large bowl and add chile sauce to taste. Season with salt and pepper to taste.

3 Spread the tomato and kidney bean mixture evenly over each pizza crust to cover, leaving a narrow rim.

4 Top each pizza with the onion and sprinkle with some grated Colby cheese and a few slices of fresh green chile to taste.

5 Bake in a preheated oven, 425°F/220°C, for about 20 minutes, until the vegetables are tender, the cheese has melted, and the dough is crisp and golden.

6 Remove the pizzas from the cookie sheet and transfer to serving plates.

NUTRITION

Calories *350*; Sugars *8 g*; Protein *18 g*; Carbohydrate *49 g*; Fat *10 g*; Saturates *3 g*

easy
10 mins
20 mins

COOK'S TIP

Serve a Mexican-style salad with this pizza. Arrange sliced tomatoes, fresh cilantro leaves, and a few slices of a small, ripe avocado on a platter. Sprinkle with fresh lime juice and coarse sea salt.

These pizza dough Italian pasties are best served hot with a salad for a delicious lunch or supper dish.

Potato *and* Tomato Calzone

1 To make the dough, strain the flour into a large mixing bowl and stir in the yeast. Make a well in the center of the mixture. Stir in the vegetable bouillon, honey, and caraway seeds, and bring the mixture together to form a dough.

2 Turn the dough out onto a lightly floured counter and knead for 8 minutes, until smooth. Place the dough in a lightly oiled mixing bowl, then cover and leave to rise in a warm place for 1 hour, or until doubled in size.

3 Meanwhile, make the filling. Heat the oil in a skillet and add all the remaining ingredients, except the cheese. Cook for about 5 minutes, stirring.

4 Divide the risen dough into 4 pieces. On a lightly floured counter, roll each piece into a 7-inch/18-cm circle. Spoon equal amounts of the filling on to one half of each circle. Sprinkle the cheese over the filling. Brush the edge of the dough with milk and fold the dough over to form 4 semi-circles, pressing to seal the edges.

5 Place on a non-stick cookie sheet and brush with milk. Cook in a preheated oven, 425°F/220°C, for 30 minutes, until golden and risen.

SERVES 4

dough

4 cups white bread flour
1 tsp rapid-rise dry yeast
1¼ cups Fresh Vegetable Bouillon (see page 14)
1 tbsp clear honey
1 tsp caraway seeds
skim milk, for glazing

filling

1 tbsp vegetable oil
1⅓ cups diced waxy potatoes
1 onion, halved and sliced
2 garlic cloves, crushed
1½ oz/40 g sun-dried tomatoes
2 tbsp chopped fresh basil
2 tbsp tomato paste
2 celery stalks, sliced
½ cup grated mozzarella cheese

NUTRITION

Calories *524*; Sugars *8 g*; Protein *17 g*; Carbohydrate *103 g*; Fat *8 g*; Saturates *2 g*

 challenging

1 hr 30 mins

35 mins

This is a variation of beef hash, which was made with salt beef and leftovers and served to sea-faring New Englanders.

Potato Hash

SERVES 4

2 tbsp butter
1 red onion, halved and sliced
1 carrot, diced
1 oz/25 g green beans, halved
generous 5 cups diced waxy potatoes
½ cup all-purpose flour
1¼ cups Fresh Vegetable Bouillon (see page 14)
8 oz/225 g bean curd, diced
salt and pepper
chopped fresh parsley, to garnish

1 Melt the butter in a large, heavy-based skillet. Add the onion, carrot, green beans, and potatoes, and cook over a fairly low heat, stirring constantly, for about 5–7 minutes, or until the vegetables begin to turn golden brown.

2 Add the flour to the skillet and cook, stirring constantly, for 1 minute. Gradually pour in the bouillon, stirring constantly.

3 Reduce the heat to low and simmer for 15 minutes, or until the vegetables and potatoes are tender.

4 Add the bean curd to the pan and cook for another 5 minutes. Season with salt and pepper to taste.

5 Sprinkle the parsley over the top to garnish and serve hot straight from the skillet.

NUTRITION

Calories *302*; Sugars *5 g*; Protein *15 g*; Carbohydrate *40 g*; Fat *10 g*; Saturates *4 g*

 easy

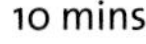 10 mins

30 mins

COOK'S TIP

A traditional hash dish is always made from chopped fresh ingredients, such as roast or corned beef, bell peppers, onion, and celery.

An assortment of vegetables is cooked with tender rice, flavored and colored with bright yellow turmeric and other warming Indian spices.

Biryani *with* Onions

1 Place the rice, lentils, bay leaf, spices, onion, cauliflower, carrot, peas, and golden raisins in a large pan. Season with salt and pepper to taste and mix well until combined.

2 Pour in the bouillon, then bring to a boil. Reduce the heat, cover, and simmer for 15 minutes, stirring occasionally, until the rice is tender. Remove from the heat and set aside, covered, for 10 minutes to let the bouillon be absorbed. Remove and discard the bay leaf, cardamom pods, cloves, and cinnamon.

3 Heat the oil in a skillet and cook the onions over medium heat for 3–4 minutes, until just softened. Add the superfine sugar, increase the heat, and cook, stirring constantly, for a further 2–3 minutes, until the onions are golden.

4 Gently combine the rice and vegetables and transfer to warm serving plates. Spoon over the caramelized onions and serve immediately with plain, warm nan bread.

SERVES 4

scant 1 cup basmati rice, rinsed
1/4 cup red lentils, rinsed
1 bay leaf
6 cardamom pods, split
1 tsp ground turmeric
6 whole cloves
1 tsp cumin seeds
1 cinnamon stick, broken
1 onion, chopped
8 oz/225 g cauliflower, broken into small florets
1 large carrot, diced
scant 1 cup frozen peas
1/3 cup golden raisins
2 1/2 cups Fresh Vegetable Bouillon (see page 14)
salt and pepper
nan bread, to serve

caramelized onions

2 tsp vegetable oil
1 red onion, shredded
1 onion, shredded
2 tsp superfine sugar

NUTRITION

Calories *223*; Sugars *18 g*; Protein *8 g*; Carbohydrate *42 g*; Fat *4 g*; Saturates *1 g*

easy

20 mins

30 mins

Vegetables are cooked in a mildly spiced curry sauce with yogurt and fresh cilantro stirred in just before serving.

Creamy Vegetable Curry

SERVES 4

2 tbsp sunflower oil
1 onion, sliced
2 tsp cumin seeds
2 tbsp ground coriander
1 tsp ground turmeric
2 tsp ground ginger
1 tsp chopped fresh red chile
2 garlic cloves, chopped
2 cups canned chopped tomatoes
3 tbsp powdered coconut mixed with 1¼ cups boiling water
1 small cauliflower, broken into florets
2 zucchini, sliced
2 carrots, sliced
1 potato, diced
1½ cups canned garbanzo beans, drained and rinsed
½ cup thick plain yogurt
2 tbsp mango chutney
3 tbsp chopped fresh cilantro
salt and pepper
fresh herbs, to garnish
cooked rice, to serve

NUTRITION

Calories *423*; Sugars *24 g*; Protein *16 g*; Carbohydrate *50 g*; Fat *19 g*; Saturates *7 g*

very easy

15 mins

20 mins

1 Heat the oil in a pan and cook the onion until soft. Add the cumin, ground coriander, turmeric, ginger, chile, and garlic and cook for 1 minute.

2 Add the tomatoes and the coconut mixture and mix well.

3 Add the cauliflower, zucchini, carrots, potato, and garbanzo beans, and season with salt and pepper to taste. Cover and simmer for 20 minutes, until the vegetables are tender.

4 Stir in the yogurt, mango chutney, and fresh cilantro and heat through gently, but do not boil.

5 Transfer to a warm serving dish, garnish with fresh herbs, and serve with rice.

COOK'S TIP

You can use dried garbanzo beans, soaked overnight, drained and cooked, but the canned variety is just as good. Vary the beans, if wished.

This recipe would make a stunning dinner party dish, served with a fresh tomato salad.

Eggplant Pasta Cake

1 Grease and line an 8-inch/20-cm round spring-form cake pan.

2 Place the eggplant in a bowl, sprinkle with salt, and let stand for 30 minutes to remove any bitter juices. Rinse well under cold running water and drain.

3 Bring a pan of water to a boil and blanch the eggplant slices for 1 minute. Drain and pat dry with paper towels. Set aside.

4 Bring a large pan of lightly salted water to a boil. Add the pasta shapes, return to a boil, and cook for 8–10 minutes, until tender, but still firm to the bite. Drain well and return to the pan. Add the soft cheese and allow it to melt over the pasta.

5 Stir in the crushed tomatoes, Parmesan, and oregano, and season with salt and pepper to taste . Set aside.

6 Arrange the eggplant slices over the bottom and sides of the cake pan, overlapping them and leaving no gaps. Pile the pasta mixture into the pan, packing it down, and sprinkle with the bread crumbs. Bake in a preheated oven, 375°F/190°C, for 20 minutes. Remove from the oven and let stand for 15 minutes.

7 Loosen the cake round the edge with a spatula and release from the pan. Turn out the pasta cake, eggplant side uppermost, and serve hot with fresh tomatoes, garnished with oregano sprigs.

SERVES 4

butter, for greasing
1 eggplant, cut into 1/4-inch/5-mm thick slices
3 cups dried tricolor pasta shapes
1/2 cup low-fat soft cheese with garlic and herbs
1 1/2 cups crushed tomatoes
scant 3/4 cup freshly grated Parmesan cheese
1 1/2 tsp dried oregano
2 tbsp dry white bread crumbs
salt and pepper
tomatoes, quartered, to serve
fresh oregano sprigs, to garnish

NUTRITION

Calories *140*; Sugars *4 g*; Protein *14 g*; Carbohydrate *22 g*; Fat *7 g*; Saturates *4 g*

 challenging

55 mins

35 mins

These stewed beans form the basis of many Mexican recipes.

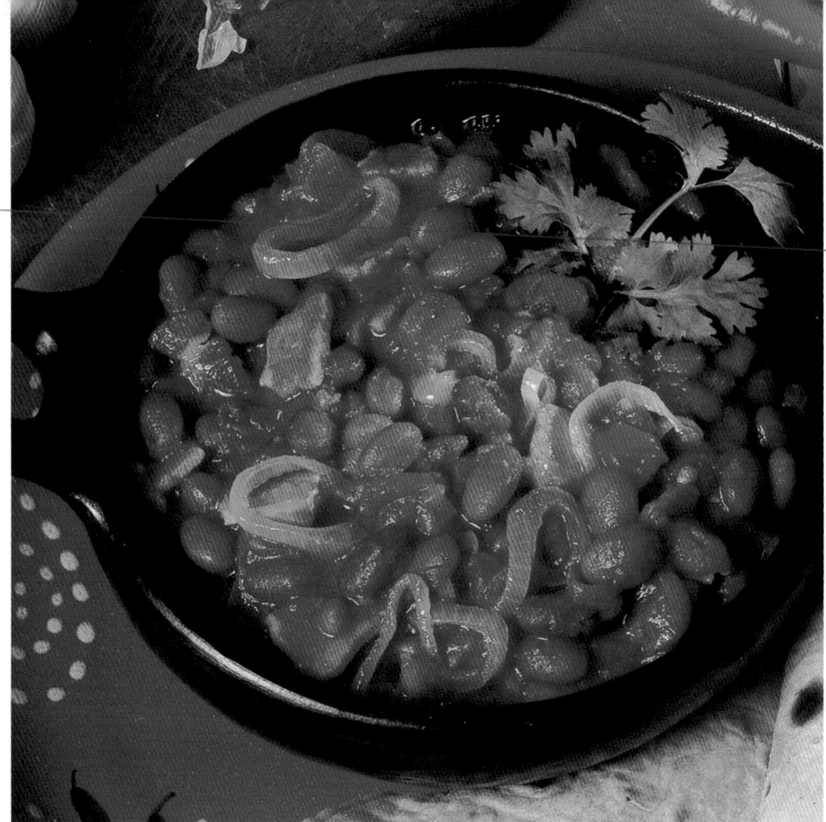

Spicy Mexican Beans

SERVES 4

8 oz/225 g dry pinto beans or cannellini beans
1 large onion, sliced
2 garlic cloves, crushed
4 cups water
salt
chopped fresh cilantro or parsley, to garnish

bean stew
2 tbsp oil
1 large onion, sliced
2 garlic cloves, crushed
8 strips lean bacon, diced
14 oz/400 g canned chopped tomatoes
1 tsp ground cumin
1 tbsp sweet chili sauce

refried beans
2 tbsp oil
1 onion, chopped
2 garlic cloves, crushed

NUTRITION
Calories *234*; Sugars *6 g*; Protein *11 g*; Carbohydrate *20 g*; Fat *13 g*; Saturates *2 g*

 easy
 8 hrs 15 mins
 4 hrs 30 mins

1 Soak the beans in a bowl of cold water overnight. Drain the beans and put into a pan with the onion, garlic, and water, then bring to a boil. Reduce the heat, cover, and simmer gently for 1½ hours. Stir well, add more boiling water, if necessary, and simmer, covered, for a further 1–1½ hours. or until the beans are tender.

2 When the beans are tender, add salt to taste and continue to cook, uncovered, for about 15 minutes to let most of the liquid evaporate. Serve the basic beans hot, sprinkled with chopped cilantro. Alternatively, let cool, then store in the refrigerator for up to 1 week.

3 To make a bean stew, heat the oil in a pan and cook the onion, garlic, and bacon for 3–4 minutes. Add the remaining ingredients and the basic beans, and bring to a boil. Reduce the heat, cover and simmer for 30 minutes, then season with salt and pepper to taste.

4 To make refried beans, heat the oil in a pan and cook the onion and garlic until golden brown. Add a quarter of the basic beans with a little of their liquid and mash. Continue adding and mashing the beans, while simmering gently, until thickened. Adjust the seasoning and serve hot.

COOK'S TIP

Don't add salt until the beans are tender, since it makes them tough.

Roasting the tomatoes gives a sweeter, smoother flavor to the sauce. Italian plum or flavia tomatoes are ideal for this dish.

Basil *and* Tomato Pasta

1 Place the rosemary, garlic, and tomatoes, skin-side up, in a shallow roasting pan and drizzle over the oil.

2 Cook under a preheated broiler for 20 minutes, or until the tomato skins have become slightly charred.

3 When cool enough to handle, peel the skin from the tomatoes. Coarsely chop the tomato flesh and place in a pan.

4 Squeeze the pulp from the garlic cloves and mix with the tomato flesh and sun-dried tomato paste.

5 Stir the basil into the sauce. Season with salt and pepper to taste.

6 Cook the farfalle in a pan of boiling, lightly salted water, according to the package instructions, or until cooked through, but still it has bite. Drain the pasta thoroughly.

7 Gently heat through the tomato and basil sauce.

8 Transfer the farfalle to serving plates and serve with the sauce, garnished with basil leaves.

COOK'S TIP

This sauce tastes just as good when served cold in a pasta salad.

SERVES 4

2 fresh rosemary sprigs
2 garlic cloves, unpeeled
1 lb/450 g tomatoes, halved and seeded
1 tbsp olive oil
1 tbsp sun-dried tomato paste
12 fresh basil leaves, torn into pieces, plus extra to garnish
salt and pepper
1 lb 8 oz/675 g fresh farfalle or 12 oz/350 g dried farfalle

NUTRITION

Calories 177; Sugars *4 g*; Protein *5 g*; Carbohydrate *31 g*; Fat *4 g*; Saturates *1 g*

 moderate

15 mins

35 mins

The flavors of Mexico are echoed in this dish, in which potato slices are topped with tomatoes and chiles and served with a piquant guacamole.

Mexican Potato Salad

SERVES 4

2 lb 12 oz/1.25 kg waxy potatoes, sliced
1 ripe avocado, halved and pitted
1 tsp olive oil
1 tsp lemon juice
1 garlic clove, crushed
1 onion, chopped
2 large tomatoes, sliced
1 fresh green chile, seeded and chopped
1 yellow bell pepper, halved, seeded, and sliced
2 tbsp chopped fresh cilantro
salt and pepper
lemon wedges, to garnish

1 Cook the potato slices in a pan of boiling water for 10–15 minutes, until tender. Drain and let cool.

2 Scoop the avocado flesh into a bowl and mash with a fork

3 Add the olive oil, lemon juice, garlic, and onion to the avocado flesh and stir to combine. Cover the bowl with plastic wrap, to minimize discoloration, and set aside.

4 Mix the tomatoes, chile, and yellow bell pepper together and transfer to a salad bowl with the potato slices.

5 Arrange the avocado mixture on top of the salad and sprinkle with the chopped fresh cilantro.

6 Season the salad with salt and pepper to taste and serve garnished with the lemon wedges.

NUTRITION
Calories *260*; Sugars *6 g*; Protein *6 g*; Carbohydrate *41 g*; Fat *9 g*; Saturates *2 g*

 easy
 20 mins
 20 mins

COOK'S TIP

You can omit the green chile from this salad if you do not like hot dishes.

This salad is quite deceptive—it is, in fact, surprisingly filling, even though it looks very light.

Grapefruit *and* Coconut Salad

1 Toast the grated coconut in a dry skillet over low heat, stirring constantly, for about 3 minutes, or until it is golden brown. Transfer the toasted coconut to a bowl.

2 Add the light soy sauce, lime juice, and water to the toasted coconut and mix together well.

3 Heat the oil in a pan and sauté the garlic and onion until softened. Stir the onion into the coconut mixture. Remove and discard the garlic.

4 Divide the grapefruit segments between 4 plates. Sprinkle each with the alfalfa sprouts and spoon over the coconut mixture.

SERVES 4

1¼ cups grated coconut
2 tsp light soy sauce
2 tbsp lime juice
2 tbsp water
2 tsp sunflower oil
1 garlic clove, halved
1 onion, chopped finely
2 large ruby grapefruits, peeled and segmented
1 cup alfalfa sprouts

NUTRITION

Calories *201*; Sugars 133 *g*; Protein *3 g*; Carbohydrate *14 g*; Fat *15 g*; Saturates *9 g*

very easy

10 mins

10 mins

Serve this spicy, Indian-style rice dish with a low-fat plain yogurt raita for a delightfully refreshing contrast.

Hot *and* Spicy Rice Salad

SERVES 4

2 tsp vegetable oil
1 onion, chopped finely
1 fresh red chile, seeded and chopped finely
8 cardamom pods
1 tsp ground turmeric
1 tsp garam masala
1¾ cups basmati rice, rinsed
3 cups boiling water
1 orange bell pepper, halved, seeded, and chopped
2 cups cauliflower flowerets
4 ripe tomatoes, skinned, seeded, and chopped
scant 1 cup seedless raisins
¼ cup toasted sliced almonds
salt and pepper
raita of low-fat plain yogurt, onion, cucumber, and mint, to serve

NUTRITION
Calories *329*; Sugars *27 g*; Protein *8 g*; Carbohydrate *59 g*;Fat *8 g*; Saturates *1 g*

 easy
 30 mins
 35 mins

1 Heat the oil in a large, non-slip pan. Add the onion, chile, cardamom pods, turmeric, and garam masala and cook over low heat for 2–3 minutes, until the vegetables have softened.

2 Stir in the rice, boiling water, orange bell pepper, and cauliflower. Season with salt and pepper to taste.

3 Cover with a tight-fitting lid and bring to a boil. Reduce the heat and simmer for 15 minutes, without lifting the lid.

4 Uncover the pan and fork through the rice. Stir in the tomatoes and raisins.

5 Cover the pan again, turn off the heat, and let the rice salad stand for 15 minutes, then remove and discard the cardamom pods.

6 Pile the rice onto a warm serving platter and sprinkle with the toasted sliced almonds. Serve the rice salad with the yogurt raita.

This cooling salad is a good foil for a highly spiced meal. Omit the green chile, if preferred.

Cool Cucumber Salad

1 Arrange the cucumber slices on a round serving plate.

2 Scatter the green chile over the cucumber.

3 To make the dressing, mix together the cilantro, lemon juice, salt, and sugar.

4 Place the cucumber in the refrigerator and let chill for at least 1 hour, or until required.

5 When ready to serve, transfer the cucumber to a serving dish. Pour the salad dressing over the cucumber just before serving and garnish with fresh mint and red bell pepper strips.

SERVES 4

1 cucumber, sliced thinly
1 fresh green chile, chopped finely (optional)

to garnish

sprigs of fresh mint
red bell pepper strips

dressing

fresh cilantro leaves, chopped finely
2 tbsp lemon juice
½ tsp salt
1 tsp sugar

NUTRITION

Calories *11*; Sugars *2 g*; Protein *0.4 g*; Carbohydrate *2 g*; Fat *0 g*; Saturates *0 g*

very easy
1 hr 15 mins
0 mins

COOK'S TIP

For the best results, use a vegetable peeler to slice the cucumber thinly.

Couscous is a type of semolina made from durum wheat. It is wonderful in salads, as it readily absorbs the flavor of the dressing.

Moroccan Salad

SERVES 4

1 cup couscous
1 bunch scallions, chopped finely
1 small green bell pepper, halved seeded, and chopped
4-inch/10-cm piece of cucumber, chopped
3/4 cup canned garbanzo beans, drained and rinsed
1/2 cup golden raisins or raisins
handful of salad greens
2 oranges, peeled and segmented
salt and pepper
fresh mint sprigs, to garnish

dressing
zest of 1 orange, finely grated
1 tbsp chopped fresh mint
2/3 cup low-fat plain yogurt

1 Put the couscous into a bowl and pour boiling water over to cover. Let soak for about 15 minutes, until the grains are tender, then stir gently with a fork to separate them.

2 Add the scallions, green bell pepper, cucumber, garbanzo beans, and golden raisins to the couscous, stirring to combine. Season with salt and pepper to taste.

3 To make the dressing, place the orange peel, mint, and yogurt in a bowl and mix together until combined. Pour the dressing over the couscous and stir to mix well.

4 Arrange the salad greens on 4 serving plates. Divide the couscous mixture between the plates and arrange the orange segments on top. Garnish with fresh mint sprigs and serve.

NUTRITION
Calories *195*; Sugars *15 g*; Protein *8 g*; Carbohydrate *40 g*; Fat *2 g*; Saturates *0.3 g*

easy

 30 mins

 0 mins

Homemade coleslaw tastes far superior to any that you can buy. If you make it in advance, add the sunflower seeds just before serving.

Coleslaw

1 To make the dressing, combine the mayonnaise, yogurt, and Tabasco sauce, and season with salt and pepper to taste in a small bowl. Let chill until required.

2 Combine the cabbage, carrots, and green bell pepper in a large bowl and toss to mix. Pour the dressing over and toss until the vegetables are coated. Let chill until required.

3 Just before serving, place the sunflower seeds on a cookie sheet and toast them in the oven or under the broiler until golden brown.

4 Transfer the salad to a large serving dish, scatter with sunflower seeds, and serve.

SERVES 4

1 head of white cabbage, shredded
4 carrots, grated
1 green bell pepper, halved, seeded, and cut into thin strips
2 tbsp sunflower seeds
salt and pepper

dressing

⅔ cup low-fat mayonnaise
⅔ cup low-fat plain yogurt
dash of Tabasco sauce

NUTRITION

Calories *224*; Sugars *8 g*; Protein *3 g*; Carbohydrate *8 g*; Fat *20 g*; Saturates *3 g*

easy

10 mins

5 mins

COOK'S TIP

To give the coleslaw a slightly different flavor and texture, add one or more of the following ingredients: raisins, grapes, or grated apple.

This colorful, summery salad of crisp vegetables is tossed in a delicious sun-dried tomato dressing.

Green Bean *and* Carrot Salad

SERVES 4

12 oz/350 g green beans
8 oz/225 g carrots, cut into thin sticks
1 red bell pepper, halved, seeded, and cut into thin strips
1 red onion, thinly sliced

dressing

2 tbsp extra-virgin olive oil
1 tbsp red wine vinegar
2 tsp sun-dried tomato paste
¼ tsp superfine sugar
salt and pepper

NUTRITION

Calories *104*; Sugars *9 g*; Protein *2 g*; Carbohydrate *10 g*; Fat *6 g*; Saturates *1 g*

very easy

10 mins

5 mins

1 Blanch the green beans in boiling water for 4 minutes, until just tender. Drain the beans and rinse them under cold running water until they are cool. Drain again thoroughly.

2 Transfer the drained beans to a large salad bowl. Add the carrots, red bell pepper, and onion to the beans and toss to mix.

3 To make the dressing, place the oil, wine vinegar, sun-dried tomato paste, and sugar in a small screw-top jar and season with salt and pepper to taste. Shake vigorously to mix.

4 Pour the dressing over the vegetables and serve immediately, or let chill in the refrigerator until required.

COOK'S TIP

Use canned beans if fresh ones are unavailable. Rinse off the salty canning liquid and drain well. There is no need to blanch canned beans.

This is a refreshing and very nutritious salad. Add the dressing just before serving to prevent the leaves becoming soggy.

Spinach *and* Orange Salad

1 Slice the top and bottom off each orange with a sharp knife, then remove the peel and pith. Working over a small bowl, carefully slice between the membranes of the orange to remove the segments. Reserve any juices for the salad dressing.

2 Mix together the spinach leaves and orange segments, and arrange them in a serving dish. Sprinkle the onion over the salad.

3 To make the dressing, whisk together the olive oil, orange juice, lemon juice, honey, and mustard in a small bowl. Season with salt and pepper to taste.

4 Pour the dressing over the salad just before serving. Toss the salad well to coat the leaves with the dressing.

SERVES 4

2 large oranges
8 oz/225 g baby spinach leaves
½ red onion, chopped

dressing

3 tbsp extra-virgin olive oil
2 tbsp freshly squeezed orange juice
2 tsp lemon juice
1 tsp honey
½ tsp wholegrain mustard
salt and pepper

NUTRITION

Calories *126*; Sugars *10 g*; Protein *3 g*; Carbohydrate *10 g*; Fat *9 g*; Saturates *1 g*

very easy

10 mins

0 mins

This is a very refreshing salad. The subtle aniseed flavor of fennel combines well with the cucumber and fresh mint.

Egg *and* Fennel Salad

SERVES 4

1 fennel bulb, sliced thinly
lemon juice
2 small oranges
1 small cucumber, cut into ½-inch/1-cm thick rounds, and quartered
1 tbsp chopped fresh mint
1 tbsp extra-virgin olive oil
2 hard-cooked eggs

1 Place the fennel in a bowl of water with a little lemon juice. (See Cook's Tip.)

2 Grate the peel of the oranges over a bowl. Using a sharp knife, pare away the orange peel, then segment the orange by carefully slicing between each line of pith. Do this over the bowl to retain the juice.

3 Drain the fennel and mix with the orange segments and juice, cucumber and mint, and mix gently to combine.

4 Pour the olive oil over the fennel and cucumber salad and toss well.

5 Peel and quarter the hard-cooked eggs and use to decorate the top of the salad. Serve at once.

NUTRITION

Calories *90*; Sugars *7 g*; Protein *4 g*; Carbohydrate *7 g*; Fat *5 g*; Saturates *1 g*

very easy

25 mins

0 mins

COOK'S TIP

Fennel discolors if it is left for any length of time without a dressing. To prevent any discoloration, place it in a bowl of water with a little lemon juice.

The sweetness of the pear is a perfect partner to the peppery "bite" of the radicchio and the piquancy of the cheese.

Pear *and* Roquefort Salad

1 Place the cheese in a bowl and mash with a fork. Gradually blend the yogurt into the cheese to make a smooth dressing. Add the chives and season with pepper to taste.

2 Arrange the salad greens on a large serving platter or divide them between individual serving plates.

3 Arrange the pear slices over the salad leaves. Drizzle the Roquefort dressing over the pears and garnish with a few whole chives.

SERVES 4

2 oz/55 g Roquefort cheese
⅔ cup low-fat plain yogurt
2 tbsp chopped fresh chives
few lollo rosso leaves
few radicchio leaves
few mâche leaves
2 ripe pears, cored and thinly sliced
pepper
whole fresh chives, to garnish

COOK'S TIP

Look out for bags of mixed salad greens, as these are generally more economical than buying lots of different types of salad greens separately.

NUTRITION

Calories *94*; Sugars *10 g*; Protein *5 g*; Carbohydrate *10 g*; Fat *4 g*; Saturates *3 g*

 very easy

10 mins

 0 mins

Desserts

One of the healthiest endings to a meal is fresh fruit topped with low-fat plain yogurt or fromage frais. Fruit contains no fat and is naturally rich in vitamins and fibre—perfect for a low-fat diet! However, there are many other ways to use fruit as the basis of a range of delicious desserts. Experiment with the unusual and exotic fruits that are increasingly available in our super stores. In this chapter there is a mouth-watering range of hot and cold fruit desserts, sophisticated mousses, and satisfying cakes, as well as variations on the traditional fruit salad. There are also a number of non-fruit based desserts, such as New Age Spotted Dick and Almond Trifle, and even some low-fat treats for chocoholics, such as the super-light Chocolate Cheese Pots and Mocha Swirl Mousse.

A wonderful mixture of summer fruits encased in slices of white bread, which soak up the deep red, flavorful juices.

Summer Puddings

SERVES 4

butter or vegetable oil, for greasing
6–8 thin slices of white bread, crusts removed
¾ cup superfine sugar
1¼ cups water
8 oz/225 g strawberries
1 lb 2 oz/500 g raspberries
1¼ cups blackcurrants and/or redcurrants
1½ cups blackberries or loganberries
fresh mint sprigs, to decorate
pouring cream, to serve

NUTRITION
Calories *174*; Sugars *42 g*; Protein *2 g*; Carbohydrate *43 g*; Fat *0 g*; Saturates *0 g*

moderate
8 hrs 10 mins
10 mins

1 Grease 6 x ⅔ cup molds with a little butter. Line the molds with the bread, cutting it so it fits snugly.

2 Place the sugar in a pan with the water and heat gently, stirring frequently until dissolved, then bring to a boil and cook for 2 minutes.

3 Reserve 6 large strawberries for decoration. Add half the raspberries and the rest of the fruits to the syrup, cutting the strawberries in half, if large. Reduce the heat and simmer gently for a few minutes, until they begin to soften, but still retain their shape.

4 Spoon the fruits and some of the liquid into the molds. Cover with more slices of bread. Spoon a little juice over the molds so the bread is well soaked. Cover each mold with a saucer and a heavy weight, let cool, then chill thoroughly, preferably overnight.

5 Process the remaining raspberries in a food processor or blender, or press through a nonmetallic strainer. Add enough of the liquid from the fruits to give a coating consistency.

6 Turn onto serving plates and spoon the raspberry sauce over. Decorate with the mint sprigs and reserved strawberries and serve with cream.

This is like a summer pudding, but it uses fruits which appear later in the year. This dessert requires chilling overnight so prepare in advance.

Fall Fruit Bread Pudding

SERVES 4

2 lb/900 g mixed fruit, including blackberries, apples, and pears, chopped
1 cup soft light brown sugar
1 tsp ground cinnamon
7 tbsp water
8 oz/225 g white bread, sliced thinly, crusts removed (about 12 slices)

1 Place the fruit in a large pan with the soft light brown sugar, cinnamon, and water, stir, and bring to a boil. Reduce the heat and simmer for 5–10 minutes, until the fruits have softened, but still hold their shape.

2 Meanwhile, line the bottom and sides of a 3¾ cup heatproof bowl with the bread slices, ensuring that there are no gaps between the pieces of bread.

3 Spoon the fruit and some of the juices into the center of the bread-lined bowl and cover the fruit with the remaining bread. Spoon the rest of the juices over the bread.

4 Place a saucer on top of the pudding and place a heavy weight on it. Chill the pudding in the refrigerator overnight.

5 When ready to serve the pudding, turn it out on to a serving plate.

NUTRITION

Calories *178*; Sugars 31 *g*; Protein *3 g*; Carbohydrate *42 g*; Fat *1 g*; Saturates *0.1 g*

easy

8 hrs 10 mins

10 mins

COOK'S TIP

This pudding is delicious served with low-fat vanilla ice cream, which counteracts the tartness of the blackberries. Stand the pudding on a plate when chilling to catch any juices that run down the sides of the basin.

An interesting alternative to the familiar and ever-popular summer dessert that uses dried fruits and a tasty malt loaf.

Winter Puddings

SERVES 4

- scant 3/4 cup coarsely chopped, ready-to-eat dried apricots,
- 6 cups coarsely chopped dried apple
- generous 1 3/4 cups orange juice
- 1 tsp grated orange rind, plus extra to decorate
- 2 tbsp orange liqueur
- 11 1/2 oz/325 g fruit malt loaf, cut into 1/2-inch/5-mm thick slices
- low-fat plain yogurt or low-fat crème fraîche, to serve

1 Place the apricots, apple, and orange juice in a pan, then bring to a boil. Reduce the heat and simmer for 10 minutes. Remove the fruit, using a draining spoon, and reserve the liquid. Place the fruit in a dish and set aside to cool. Stir in the orange rind and orange liqueur.

2 Line 4 x 3/4 cup bowls or ramekin dishes with baking parchment.

3 Cut 4 circles from the malt loaf slices to fit the tops of the molds and cut the remaining slices to line them.

4 Soak the malt loaf slices in the reserved fruit syrup, then arrange around the bottom and sides of the molds. Trim away any crusts which overhang the edges. Fill the centers with the chopped fruit, pressing down well, and place the malt loaf circles on top.

5 Cover with baking parchment and weigh each bowl down with an 8 oz/225 g weight or a food can. Let chill in the refrigerator overnight.

6 Remove the weight and baking parchment. Carefully turn the puddings out onto 4 serving plates. Remove the lining paper.

7 Decorate with orange rind and serve with a spoonful of yogurt.

NUTRITION

Calories *447*; Sugars *68 g*; Protein *9 g*; Carbohydrate *80 g*; Fat *11 g*; Saturates *5 g*

easy

 8 hrs 15 mins

 15 mins

The sugar lumps give a lovely crunchy topping to this easy blackberry and apple dessert.

Crispy-topped Fruit Bake

1 Grease and line a 2 lb/900 g loaf pan with a little butter. Place the cooking apples in a pan with the lemon juice, then bring to a boil. Reduce the heat, cover, and simmer for about 10 minutes, until softened and pulpy. Beat well and set aside to cool.

2 Strain the flour, baking powder, and cinnamon into a bowl, adding any husks that remain in the strainer. Stir in ½ cup of the blackberries and the sugar.

3 Make a well in the center of the ingredients and add the egg, yogurt, and cooled apple purée. Mix well to incorporate thoroughly. Spoon the mixture into the prepared loaf pan and smooth the top.

4 Sprinkle with the remaining blackberries, pressing them down into the cake batter, and top with the crushed sugar lumps. Bake in a preheated oven, 375°F/190°C, for 40–45 minutes. Remove from the oven and set aside in the pan to cool.

5 Remove the cake from the pan and peel away the lining paper. Serve dusted with cinnamon and decorated with extra blackberries and apple slices.

COOK'S TIP

Try replacing the blackberries with blueberries. Use the canned or frozen variety if fresh blueberries are unavailable.

SERVES 10

butter or margarine, for greasing
12 oz/350 g tart cooking apples, peeled, cored, and diced
3 tbsp lemon juice
2½ cups self-rising whole-wheat flour
½ tsp baking powder
1 tsp ground cinnamon, plus extra for dusting
¾ cup blackberries, thawed if frozen, plus extra to decorate
¾ cup molasses sugar
1 egg, beaten
scant 1 cup low-fat plain yogurt
2 oz/55 g white or brown sugar lumps, crushed lightly
dessert apple, sliced, to decorate

NUTRITION

Calories *227*; Sugars *30 g*; Protein *5 g*; Carbohydrate *53 g*; Fat *1 g*; Saturates *0.2 g*

 moderate

 15 mins

 55 mins

This sweet, fruity loaf is ideal served with coffee for a healthy snack. The fruit spread can be made quickly while the cake is baking in the oven.

Fruit Loaf *with* Apple Spread

SERVES 8

butter or margarine, for greasing
1¾ cups rolled oats
scant ½ cup molasses sugar
1 tsp ground cinnamon
scant 1 cup golden raisins
generous 1 cup seedless raisins
2 tbsp malt extract
1¼ cups unsweetened apple juice
1½ cups self-rising whole-wheat flour
1½ tsp baking powder

to serve
strawberries, halved
apple wedges

fruit spread
2 dessert apples, cored and chopped
1 tbsp lemon juice
2 cups strawberries, washed and hulled
1¼ cups unsweetened apple juice

1. Grease and line a 2 lb/900 g loaf pan and set aside. Place the oats, sugar, cinnamon, golden raisins, raisins, and malt extract in a mixing bowl. Pour in the apple juice, stir well, and set aside to soak for 30 minutes.
2. Sift in the flour and baking powder, adding any husks that remain in the strainer, and fold in using a metal spoon. Spoon the batter into the prepared pan and bake in a preheated oven, 350°F/180°C, for 1½ hours, until firm or until a toothpick inserted into the center comes out clean.
3. Remove the pan from the oven and place on a wire rack to cool for about 10 minutes, then turn the loaf out onto the rack and set aside to cool.
4. Meanwhile, make the fruit spread. Toss the apples in the lemon juice and place in a pan with the strawberries. Pour in the apple juice, then bring to a boil. Reduce the heat, cover, and simmer for 30 minutes. Beat the sauce well and spoon into a clean, warm jar. Set aside to cool, then seal, and label.
5. Serve the loaf with the fruit spread, strawberries, and apple wedges.

NUTRITION
Calories *733*; Sugars *110 g*; Protein *12 g*; Carbohydrate *171 g*; Fat *5 g*; Saturates *1 g*

moderate

1 hr 15 mins

2 hrs

This is a deliciously moist low-fat pudding. The sauce is in the center of the pudding, and oozes out when it is cut.

New Age Spotted Dick

SERVES 4

1 cup raisins
½ cup water
½ cup corn oil, plus a little for brushing
½ cup superfine sugar
⅓ cup ground almonds
2 eggs, lightly beaten
scant 1½ cups self-rising flour

sauce

½ cup walnuts, chopped
⅔ cup ground almonds
1¼ cups semi-skim milk
4 tbsp granulated sugar

1. Put the raisins in a pan with the water. Bring to a boil, then remove from the heat. Let steep for 10 minutes, then drain.
2. Whisk together the oil, sugar, and ground almonds until thick and syrupy; this will take about 8 minutes on medium speed if using an electric whisk. Add the eggs, one at a time, beating well after each addition. Combine the flour and raisins. Stir into the mixture.
3. Brush a 4 cup/1 liter heatproof bowl with oil, or line with baking parchment.
4. Put all the sauce ingredients into a pan. Bring to a boil, stir, then reduce the heat and simmer for 10 minutes.
5. Transfer the sponge mixture to the greased bowl and pour the hot sauce over the top. Place the bowl on a cookie sheet.
6. Bake in a preheated oven, 340°F/ 170°C, for about 1 hour, or until well risen. Lay a piece of baking parchment across the top of the pudding if it starts to brown too quickly.
7. Let cool for 2–3 minutes in the bowl before turning it out onto a warm serving plate.

COOK'S TIP

Always soak raisins before baking them, as they plump up nicely and do not dry out during cooking.

NUTRITION

Calories *529*; Sugars *41 g*; Protein *9 g*; Carbohydrate *58 g*; Fat *31 g*; Saturates *4 g*

 easy

 25 mins

1 hr 15 mins

Serve this moist, fruit-laden cake for a special occasion. It would also make an excellent Thanksgiving cake.

Rich Fruit Cake

SERVES 8

butter or margarine, for greasing
6 oz/175 g unsweetened stoned dates, chopped
½ cup ready-to-eat dried prunes, chopped
scant 1 cup unsweetened orange juice
2 tbsp molasses
1 tsp finely grated lemon peel
1 tsp finely grated orange peel
2 cups self-rising whole-wheat flour
1 tsp apple spice
scant 1 cup seedless raisins
scant 1 cup golden raisins
½ cup currants
1 cup dried cranberries
3 large eggs, separated

to decorate

1 tbsp apricot jelly, warmed
confectioners' sugar, to dust
generous 1 cup sugarpaste
strips of orange peel
strips of lemon peel

NUTRITION

Calories *772*; Sugars *137 g*; Protein *14 g*; Carbohydrate *179 g*; Fat *5 g*; Saturates *1 g*

 moderate
35 mins
1 hr 45 mins

1 Grease and line a deep 8-inch/20-cm round cake pan. Place the dates and prunes in a pan. Pour the orange juice over and simmer for 10 minutes. Remove the pan from the heat and beat the fruit mixture until puréed. Add the molasses and lemon and orange rinds. Set aside to cool.

2 Sift the flour and spice into a bowl, adding any husks from the strainer. Add the dried fruits.

3 When the date and prune mixture is cool, whisk in the egg yolks. Spoon the fruit mixture into the dry ingredients and mix together.

4 In a clean bowl, whisk the egg whites until stiff and gently fold them into the cake batter. Transfer to the prepared pan and bake in a preheated oven, 325°F/170°C, for 1½ hours. Set aside to cool.

5 Remove the cake from the pan and brush the top with jelly. Dust the counter with confectioners' sugar and roll out the sugarpaste thinly. Lay it over the top of the cake and trim the edges. Decorate with orange and lemon peel.

This melt-in-your-mouth version of a favorite cake has a fraction of the fat of the traditional version.

Carrot *and* Ginger Cake

1 Grease and line an 8-inch/20-cm round cake pan with baking parchment.

2 Strain the flour, baking powder, baking soda, ground ginger, and salt into a bowl. Stir in the sugar, carrots, preserved ginger, gingerroot, and raisins.

3 Beat together the eggs, oil, and orange juice, then pour into the bowl. Mix the ingredients together well.

4 Spoon the cake batter into the pan and bake in a preheated oven, 350°F/180°C, for 1–1¼ hours, until firm to the touch or until a skewer inserted into the center of the cake comes out clean.

5 To make the frosting, place the soft cheese in a bowl and beat to soften. Sift in the confectioners' sugar and add the vanilla extract. Mix well.

6 Remove the cake from the pan and smooth the frosting over the top. Decorate the cake with the carrot and ginger and serve.

SERVES 10

butter or margarine, for greasing
1¾ cups all-purpose flour
1 tsp baking powder
1 tsp baking soda
2 tsp ground ginger
½ tsp salt
¾ cup molasses sugar
1⅔ cups grated carrots
2 pieces chopped preserved ginger
1 tbsp grated fresh gingerroot
generous ⅓ cup seedless raisins
2 eggs, beaten
3 tbsp corn oil
juice of 1 orange

frosting

1 cup low-fat soft cheese
4 tbsp confectioners' sugar
1 tsp vanilla extract

to decorate

carrot, grated
preserved ginger, grated
ground ginger

NUTRITION

Calories *249*; Sugars *28 g*; Protein *7 g*; Carbohydrate *46 g*; Fat *6 g*; Saturates *1 g*

 moderate
15 mins
1 hr 15 mins

COOK'S TIP

You could serve this hot or cold, but the cake improves after a day or two.

A substantial cake that is ideal served with coffee. The mashed bananas help to keep the cake moist, and the lime frosting gives it extra zest.

Banana *and* Lime Cake

SERVES 10

butter or margarine, for greasing
generous 2 cups all-purpose flour
1 tsp salt
1½ tsp baking powder
scant 1 cup light brown sugar
1 tsp grated lime peel
1 egg, beaten lightly
1 banana, mashed with 1 tbsp lime juice
⅔ cup low-fat plain yogurt
⅔ cup golden raisins

topping
generous 1 cup confectioners' sugar
1–2 tsp lime juice
½ tsp finely grated lime peel

to decorate
banana chips
finely grated lime peel

1 Grease a deep round 7-inch/18-cm cake pan with butter and line with baking parchment.

2 Strain the flour, salt, and baking powder into a mixing bowl and stir in the sugar and lime peel.

3 Make a well in the center of the dry ingredients and add the egg, banana, yogurt, and golden raisins. Mix well until thoroughly incorporated.

4 Spoon the cake batter into the pan and smooth the surface. Bake in a preheated oven, 350°F/180°C, for 40–45 minutes, until firm to the touch or until a skewer inserted into the center comes out clean. Let cool in the pan for 10 minutes, then turn out onto a wire rack.

5 To make the topping, strain the confectioners' sugar into a small bowl and mix with the lime juice to form a soft, but not too runny frosting. Stir in the lime peel. Drizzle the lime frosting over the top of the cake, letting it run down the sides.

6 Decorate the cake with banana chips and lime peel. Before serving, let the cake stand for 15 minutes to allow the frosting to set.

NUTRITION
Calories *235*; Sugars *31 g*; Protein *5 g*; Carbohydrate *55 g*; Fat *1 g*; Saturates *0.3 g*

 easy
35 mins
45 mins

Serve this moist, light sponge cake rolled up with a creamy almond and strawberry filling for a delicious dessert.

Strawberry Roulade

1 Line a 14 x 10-inch/35 x 25-cm jelly roll pan with baking parchment.

2 Place the eggs in a heatproof bowl with the superfine sugar. Place the bowl over a pan of hot water and whisk until pale and thick.

3 Remove the bowl from the pan. Strain in the flour and fold into the eggs along with the hot water. Pour the cake batter into the pan and bake in a preheated oven, 425°F/220°C, for 8–10 minutes, until golden and set.

4 Turn out the cake onto a sheet of baking paper. Peel off the lining paper and roll up the sponge cake tightly along with the baking parchment. Wrap in a dish cloth and let cool.

5 Mix together the mascarpone and the almond extract. Chill the mascarpone mixture and the sliced strawberries in the refrigerator until required.

6 Unroll the cake, spread the mascarpone mixture over the surface, and sprinkle with sliced strawberries. Roll the cake up again and transfer to a serving plate. Sprinkle with almonds and lightly dust with confectioners' sugar. Decorate with the reserved strawberries.

SERVES 8

3 large eggs
⅔ cup superfine sugar
scant 1 cup all-purpose flour
1 tbsp hot water

filling

¾ cup low-fat mascarpone
1 tsp almond extract
1½ cups small strawberries, hulled and sliced

to decorate

1 tbsp slivered almonds, toasted
1 tsp confectioners' sugar
a few strawberries

NUTRITION

Calories *166*; Sugars *19 g*; Protein *6 g*; Carbohydrate *30 g*; Fat *3 g*; Saturates *1 g*

 challlenging

30 mins

10 mins

The perfect choice for people on a low-fat diet, these little cakes contain no butter, just a little corn oil and plenty of fruit.

Fruity Muffins

SERVES 10

$1\frac{3}{4}$ cups self-rising whole-wheat flour
2 tsp baking powder
2 tbsp molasses sugar
$3\frac{1}{4}$ cup ready-to-eat dried apricots, chopped finely
1 banana, mashed with 1 tbsp orange juice
1 tsp finely grated orange zest
$1\frac{1}{4}$ cups skim milk
1 egg, beaten
3 tbsp corn oil
2 tbsp rolled oats
fruit spread, honey, or maple syrup, to serve

1 Place 10 paper muffin cases in a deep patty pan. Strain the flour and baking powder into a mixing bowl, adding any husks that remain in the strainer. Stir in the sugar and chopped apricots.

2 Make a well in the center and add the banana, orange zest, milk, beaten egg, and oil. Mix together well to form a thick batter. Divide the batter evenly among the 10 paper cases.

3 Sprinkle with a few rolled oats and bake in a preheated oven, 400°F/200°C, for 25–30 minutes, until well risen and firm to the touch or until a skewer inserted into the center comes out clean.

4 Transfer the muffins to a wire rack to cool slightly.

5 Serve the muffins while still warm with a little fruit spread.

NUTRITION
Calories *162*; Sugars *11 g*; Protein *4 g*; Carbohydrate *28 g*; Fat *4 g*; Saturates *1 g*

very easy
10 mins
25–30 mins

COOK'S TIP

If you like dried figs, they make a deliciously crunchy alternative to the apricots; they also go very well with the flavor of orange. Other finely chopped, ready-to-eat dried fruits can be used as well.

This simple, healthy recipe is easy to prepare and cook, but is deliciously satisfying. For a treat, serve on a pool of low-fat custard.

Baked Pears *with* Cinnamon

1 Brush the pears with the lemon juice to prevent them from discoloring. Place the pears, cored-side down, in a small, non-slip roasting pan.

2 Place the sugar, cinnamon, and low-fat spread in a small pan and heat gently, stirring constantly, until the sugar has dissolved. Keep the heat very low to prevent the water evaporating from the low-fat spread as it gets hot. Spoon the mixture over the pears.

3 Bake the pears in a preheated oven, 400°F/200°C, for 20–25 minutes, or until they are tender and golden, occasionally spooning the sugar mixture over the fruit.

4 To serve, heat the low-fat custard in a small pan over low heat, or in a bowl in the microwave, until it is piping hot. Spoon a little over the surface of each of 4 warm dessert plates, then arrange 2 pear halves on each one.

5 Decorate the pears with a little lemon peel and serve immediately.

SERVES 4

4 ripe pears, peeled, cored, and halved lengthwise
2 tbsp lemon juice
¼ cup molasses sugar
1 tsp ground cinnamon
¼ cup low-fat spread
low-fat custard, to serve
finely shredded lemon peel, to decorate

COOK'S TIP

For alternative flavors, replace the cinnamon with ground ginger and serve the pears sprinkled with chopped preserved ginger in syrup. Alternatively, use ground allspice and spoon over some warm dark rum before serving.

NUTRITION

Calories *207*; Sugars *35 g*; Protein *3 g*; Carbohydrate *37 g*; Fat *6 g*; Saturates *2 g*

very easy

10 mins
25 mins

These fruity little desserts are really easy to make. Serve the jell-o with low-fat ice cream and be transported back to childhood!

Apricot *and* Orange Jell-o

SERVES 4

1½ cups ready-to-eat dried apricots
1¼ cups unsweetened orange juice
2 tbsp lemon juice
2–3 tsp clear honey
1 tbsp powdered gelozone
4 tbsp boiling water

to decorate

orange segments
fresh mint sprigs

cinnamon "cream"

½ cup medium-fat ricotta cheese
½ cup low-fat plain yogurt
1 tsp ground cinnamon, plus extra to decorate
1 tbsp clear honey

1 Place the apricots in a pan and pour in the orange juice, then bring to a boil, Reduce the heat, cover, and simmer for 15–20 minutes, until the apricots are plump and soft. Let cool for 10 minutes.

2 Transfer the mixture to a blender or food processor and blend until smooth. Stir in the lemon juice and add the honey. Pour the mixture into a measuring pitcher and make up to 2½ cups with cold water.

3 Dissolve the gelozone in the boiling water and stir it into the apricot mixture in the pitcher.

4 Pour the mixture into 4 individual molds, each ⅝ cup/150 ml, or into 1 large mold, 2½ cups/600 ml. Let chill until set.

5 Meanwhile, make the cinnamon "cream." Mix all the ingredients together in a bowl. Cover the mixture and let chill until needed.

6 To turn out the jell-o, dip the molds in hot water for a few seconds and invert onto serving plates.

7 Decorate the jell-o with the orange segments and mint sprigs. Serve with the cinnamon "cream," dusted with a little extra cinnamon.

NUTRITION

Calories *206*; Sugars *36 g*; Protein *8 g*; Carbohydrate *36 g*; Fat *5 g*; Saturates *3 g*

 easy

 4 hrs 15 mins

25 mins

These tasty morsels are a real treat. Pieces of banana are dipped in caramel and then sprinkled with a few sesame seeds.

Sticky Sesame Bananas

1 Place the bananas in a bowl, spoon over the lemon juice, and stir well to coat—this will help to prevent them discoloring.

2 Place the sugar and water in a small pan and heat gently, stirring constantly, until the sugar dissolves. Bring to a boil and cook for 5–6 minutes, until the mixture turns golden brown.

3 Meanwhile, drain the bananas and blot with paper towels to dry. Line a cookie sheet or board with baking parchment and arrange the bananas, well spaced apart, on top.

4 When the caramel is ready, drizzle it over the bananas, working quickly because the caramel sets almost instantly. Sprinkle the sesame seeds over the caramelized bananas and let cool for 10 minutes.

5 Combine the yogurt, confectioners' sugar, and vanilla extract.

6 Peel the bananas from the baking parchment and arrange on serving plates. Serve the yogurt as a dip.

SERVES 4

4 ripe bananas, cut into 2-inch/5-cm pieces
3 tbsp lemon juice
generous 1 cup superfine sugar
4 tbsp cold water
2 tbsp sesame seeds
⅔ cup low-fat plain yogurt
1 tbsp confectioners' sugar
1 tsp vanilla extract

NUTRITION

Calories *215*; Sugars *38 g*; Protein *6 g*; Carbohydrate *41 g*; Fat *3 g*; Saturates *1 g*

 moderate

 15 mins

20 mins

These super-light desserts are just the thing if you have a craving for chocolate. Serve them on their own or with a selection of fruits.

Chocolate Cheese Pots

SERVES 4

$1\frac{1}{4}$ cups ricotta cheese
$\frac{2}{3}$ cup low-fat plain yogurt
2 tbsp confectioners' sugar
4 tsp low-fat drinking chocolate powder
4 tsp unsweetened cocoa
1 tsp vanilla extract
2 tbsp dark rum, optional
2 egg whites
4 chocolate cake decorations
selection of fresh fruit, to serve

1 Combine the ricotta cheese and low-fat yogurt in a bowl. Strain in the confectioners' sugar, drinking chocolate, and unsweetened cocoa and mix well. Add the vanilla extract and rum, if using.

2 In a clean bowl, whisk the egg whites until stiff. Using a metal spoon, gently fold the egg whites into the chocolate mixture.

3 Spoon the yogurt and chocolate mixture into 4 small china dessert pots and let chill in the refrigerator for about 30 minutes.

4 Decorate each chocolate cheese pot with a chocolate cake decoration and serve with an assortment of fresh fruit, such as kiwi fruit, orange, banana, strawberries, and raspberries.

NUTRITION
Calories *117*; Sugars *17 g*; Protein *9 g*; Carbohydrate *18 g*; Fat *1 g*; Saturates *1 g*

 very easy
 40 mins
0 mins

COOK'S TIP

This chocolate mixture can also be used as a cheesecake filling. Make the base with crushed amaretti cookies and egg white, and set the filling with 2 teaspoons of powdered gelozone, dissolved in 2 tablespoons of boiling water.

These trifles can be made with any type of fruit, even frozen. When they thaw the juices will soak into the biscuit base—delicious!

Almond Trifles

SERVES 4

8 amaretti cookies, crushed
4 tbsp brandy or Amaretto liqueur
1⅓ cups raspberries
1¼ cups canned low-fat custard
1¼ cups low-fat thick plain yogurt
1 tsp almond extract
2 tbsp sliced almonds, toasted
1 tsp unsweetened cocoa

1 Divide the crushed cookies between 4 serving glasses. Sprinkle over the brandy or liqueur and set aside for about 30 minutes, until softened.

2 Top with a layer of raspberries, reserving a few for decoration, and spoon over enough custard just to cover.

3 Combine the yogurt with the almond extract and spoon the mixture over the custard, smoothing the surface. Chill in the refrigerator for about 30 minutes.

4 Before serving, sprinkle with the toasted almonds and dust with unsweetened cocoa.

5 Decorate the trifles with the reserved raspberries and serve immediately.

NUTRITION

Calories *241*; Sugars *23 g*; Protein *9 g*; Carbohydrate *35 g*; Fat *6 g*; Saturates *2 g*

very easy

1 hr 15 mins

0 mins

Fruit fools are always popular, and this light, tangy version is no exception. You can use your favorite fruits in this recipe.

Tropical Fruit Fool

SERVES 4

- 1 ripe mango
- 2 kiwi fruit, peeled and chopped
- 1 banana, chopped
- 2 tbsp lime juice
- ½ tsp finely grated lime peel, plus extra to decorate
- 2 egg whites
- 15 oz/425 g canned low-fat custard
- ½ tsp vanilla extract
- 2 passion fruit, seeds scooped out (optional)

1 Peel the mango, then slice either side of the smooth, flat central pit. Roughly chop the flesh and process the fruit in a food processor or blender until smooth. Alternatively, mash with a fork.

2 Place the kiwi fruit and bananas in a bowl, and toss the fruit in the lime juice and peel.

3 In a grease-free bowl, whisk the egg whites until stiff and gently fold in the custard and vanilla extract until thoroughly mixed.

4 In 4 tall glasses, arrange alternate layers of the chopped fruit, mango purée, and custard mixture, finishing with the custard on top. Set aside to chill in the refrigerator for 20 minutes.

5 Spoon the passion fruit seeds over the fruit fools. Decorate each serving with the extra lime peel and serve.

NUTRITION
Calories *149*; Sugars *25 g*; Protein *6 g*; Carbohydrate *32 g*; Fat *0.4 g*; Saturates *0.2 g*

 easy
35 mins
 0 mins

COOK'S TIP

Other tropical fruits to try include papaya purée, with chopped pineapple and dates, or pomegranate seeds to decorate.

A zesty, creamy whip made from yogurt and milk with a hint of orange, and served with light sweet sponge cakes.

Orange Syllabub

1 Slice off the tops and bottoms of the oranges and the skin, then cut out the segments, removing the peel and membranes between each one. Divide the orange segments between 4 dessert glasses, then chill.

2 In a mixing bowl, combine the yogurt, milk powder, sugar, orange peel, and juice. Cover and chill for 1 hour. Whisk the egg whites until stiff, then fold into the yogurt mixture. Spoon on top of the orange slices and let chill for 1 hour.

3 To make the sponge hearts, line a 6 x 10-inch/15 x 25-cm baking pan with baking parchment. Whisk the eggs and superfine sugar together until thick and pale. Strain in the flours, then fold in using a large metal spoon, adding the hot water at the same time.

4 Pour the mixture into the pan and bake in a preheated oven, 425°F/220°C for 9–10 minutes, until golden on top and firm to the touch.

5 Turn the sponge out onto a sheet of baking parchment. Using a 2-inch/5-cm heart-shaped cutter, stamp out hearts. Transfer to a wire rack to cool. Lightly dust the hearts with confectioners' sugar.

6 Decorate the syllabubs with grated orange peel and serve with the sponge hearts.

SERVES 4

4 oranges
2½ cups low-fat plain yogurt
6 tbsp low-fat skim milk powder
4 tbsp superfine sugar
1 tbsp grated orange peel
4 tbsp orange juice
2 egg whites
grated orange peel, to decorate

sponge hearts

2 eggs
6 tbsp superfine sugar
⅓ cup all-purpose flour
⅓ cup whole-wheat flour
1 tbsp hot water
1 tsp confectioners' sugar

NUTRITION

Calories *464*; Sugars *74 g*; Protein *22 g*; Carbohydrate *8 g*; Fat *5 g*; Saturates *2 g*

 moderate

 2 hrs 30 mins

10 mins

Traditionally a rich mixture made with cream, this fruit-based version is just as tempting using low-fat smetana and yogurt.

Mixed Fruit Brûlées

SERVES 4

- 1 lb/450 g prepared assorted summer fruits, such as strawberries, raspberries, blackcurrants, redcurrants, and cherries, thawed if frozen
- ⅔ cup smetana
- ⅔ cup low-fat plain yogurt
- 1 tsp vanilla extract
- 4 tbsp raw sugar

1 Divide the prepared strawberries, raspberries, blackcurrants, redcurrants, and cherries between 4 small, heatproof ramekin dishes.

2 Combine the smetana, yogurt, and vanilla extract. Spoon the mixture over the fruit, to cover it completely.

3 Top each serving with 1 tablespoon raw sugar and place the desserts under a preheated broiler for 2–3 minutes, until the sugar melts and begins to caramelize. Let the brulées stand for a couple of minutes before serving, to set the topping a little.

NUTRITION

Calories *165*; Sugars *21 g*; Protein *5 g*; Carbohydrate *21 g*; Fat *7 g*; Saturates *5 g*

very easy

5 mins

5 mins

COOK'S TIP

Look out for half-fat creams, in light and heavy varieties. They are good substitutes for occasional use. Alternatively, in this recipe, double the quantity of yogurt for a lower-fat version.

This fruit meringue dish was created for Anna Pavlova, and it looks very impressive. Use fruits of your choice to make a colorful display.

Pavlova

1 Line a cookie sheet with baking parchment and mark out a 12-inch/30-cm diameter circle.

2 Whisk the egg whites and cream of tartar together until stiff. Gradually beat in the superfine sugar and vanilla extract. Whisk well until glossy and stiff.

3 Spoon or pipe the meringue mixture into the marked circle, in an even layer, slightly raised at the edges to form a dip in the center.

4 Baking the meringue depends on your preference. If you like a soft chewy meringue, bake in a preheated oven, 275°F/140°C, for about 1½ hours, until cooked, but slightly soft in the center. If you prefer a drier meringue, bake in a preheated oven, 225°F/110°C, for 3 hours, until cooked.

5 Before serving, whip the cream to a piping consistency, and either spoon or pipe on to the meringue base, leaving a border around the edge.

6 Stir the strawberries and liqueur together and spoon onto the cream. Decorate with fruits of your choice.

SERVES 4

6 egg whites
½ tsp cream of tartar
8 oz/225 g superfine sugar
1 tsp vanilla extract
1¼ cups whipping cream
2½ cups strawberries, hulled and halved
3 tbsp orange-flavoured liqueur
fruits of your choice, to decorate

NUTRITION

Calories *321*; Sugars *37 g*; Protein *3 g*; Carbohydrate *37 g*; Fat *18 g*; Saturates *11 g*

COOK'S TIP

If you like a dry meringue, you can leave it in the oven on the lowest setting overnight. However, do not use this technique with a gas oven—but in an electric oven or solid fuel cooker it is fine.

moderate

30 mins

1 hr 30 mins–3 hrs

These creamy cheese desserts are so delicious that it's hard to believe that they are low in fat.

Almond Cheesecakes

SERVES 4

12 amaretti cookies, crushed
1 egg white, beaten lightly
1 cup skim-milk soft cheese
½ tsp almond extract
½ tsp finely grated lime peel
scant ¼ cup ground almonds
2 tbsp superfine sugar
⅓ cup golden raisins
2 tsp powdered gelozone
2 tbsp boiling water
2 tbsp lime juice

to decorate
2 tbsp slivered toasted almonds
lime peel, cut into strips

1 Place the amaretti cookie crumbs in a bowl and stir in the egg white to bind them together.

2 Arrange 4 non-slip dough rings or poached egg rings, 3½-inches/9-cm across, on a cookie sheet lined with baking parchment.

3 Divide the amaretti mixture between the rings, pressing it down well. Bake in a preheated oven, 350°F/180°C, for about 10 minutes, until crisp. Remove from the oven and let cool in the rings.

4 Put the soft cheese, almond extract, lime peel, ground almonds, sugar, and golden raisins in a bowl and beat thoroughly until well mixed.

5 Dissolve the gelozone in the boiling water and stir in the lime juice. Fold into the cheese mixture and spoon over the amaretti bases. Smooth over the tops and chill for 1 hour, or until set.

6 Loosen the cheesecakes from the rings using a small spatula and transfer to serving plates. Decorate with slivered toasted almonds and strips of lime peel, and serve.

NUTRITION
Calories *361*; Sugars *29 g*; Protein *16 g*; Carbohydrate *43 g*; Fat *15 g*; Saturates *4 g*

easy

1 hr 15 mins

10 mins

A combination of feather-light yet richly moreish, these chocolate and coffee mousses are attractively presented in tall glasses.

Mocha Swirl Mousse

1 Place the coffee and chicory extract in one bowl, and the cocoa and drinking chocolate in another bowl. Divide the yogurt between the 2 bowls and mix well.

2 Dissolve the gelozone in the boiling water and set aside. In a grease-free bowl, whisk the egg whites and sugar until stiff and divide this evenly between the 2 mixtures.

3 Divide the gelozone between the 2 mixtures and, using a large metal spoon, gently fold until well mixed.

4 Spoon small amounts of the chocolate and coffee mousses alternately into 4 serving glasses and swirl together gently. Chill for 1 hour or until set.

5 To serve, top each mousse with a teaspoon of the yogurt, a chocolate coffee bean, and a light dusting of unsweetened cocoa and serve immediately.

SERVES 4

1 tbsp coffee and chicory extract
2 tsp unsweetened cocoa, plus extra for dusting
1 tsp low-fat drinking chocolate powder
⅔ cup low-fat thick plain yogurt or crème fraîche, plus 4 tsp to serve
2 tsp powdered gelozone
2 tbsp boiling water
2 large egg whites
2 tbsp superfine sugar
4 chocolate coffee beans, to serve

 COOK'S TIP

Gelozone is the vegetarian equivalent of gelatin, and is available from most health-food stores.

NUTRITION

Calories *136*; Sugars *10 g*; Protein *5 g*; Carbohydrate *11 g*; Fat *8 g*; Saturates *5 g*

 easy

 1 hr 15 mins

 0 mins

Index